THE SECRET OF REAL ESTATE REVEALED

Can You Handle the Truth?

THE SECRET OF REAL ESTATE REVEALED

DON PROCTOR

All Rights Reserved
© 2009 by Don Proctor

This book may not be reproduced in whole or in part, by any means, without written consent of the publisher.

LIFESUCCESS PUBLISHING, LLC
8900 E Pinnacle Peak Road, Suite D240
Scottsdale, AZ 85255

Telephone: 800.473.7134
Fax: 480.661.1014
E-mail: admin@lifesuccesspublishing.com

ISBN (hardcover):   978-1-59930-289-8
ISBN (e-book):   978-1-59930-290-4

Cover :   Lloyd Arbour, LifeSuccess Publishing, LLC
Layout: Daniela A. Savone, LifeSuccess Publishing, LLC

COMPANIES, ORGANIZATIONS, INSTITUTIONS, AND INDUSTRY PUBLICATIONS: Quantity discounts are available on bulk purchases of this book for reselling, educational purposes, subscription incentives, gifts, sponsorship, or fundraising. Special books or book excerpts can also be created to fit specific needs such as private labeling with your logo on the cover and a message from a VIP printed inside. For more information, please contact our Special Sales Department at LifeSuccess Publishing, LLC.

Printed in Canada

To my wife, Denice: Thank God you didn't marry one of those normal guys! And to my two sons, Stephen and Jeremy: This world we live in no longer turns without you by our sides. We are very proud of the young men you have become and of all your accomplishments.

Special Thanks

I would like to thank my cousin, Bob Proctor, for all of the training and growth principles he's taught me over the years. I'm in a much better place today due to his generous and ever-present guidance and wisdom.

Contents

Foreword	11
Acknowledgments	13
Chapter 1: It's Not Haunted	15
Chapter 2: Sticks and Stones, Baby!	25
Chapter 3: Stop Wanting—Start Earning	35
Chapter 4: Look for Rubies, not Diamonds	51
Chapter 5: Cash or Charge?	61
Chapter 6: Equity is Your Friend	71
Chapter 7: Movin' On Up	85
Chapter 8: It Ain't Hard, Just Different	101
Chapter 9: Staying Afloat	113
Chapter 10: Look, Ma, No Toupee!	125

Foreword

Mark Twain – American humorist, writer and lecturer – once said, "If you tell the truth you don't have to remember anything."

Don Proctor is the kind of talker who rarely follows a written script when he speaks. He doesn't have to "remember anything" because he speaks from experience and straight from his heart.

That is the mark of a good speaker and great human being. I have spent more than 40 years teaching people how to change their lives and what Don has to tell you in his new book, *The Secret of Real Estate Revealed: Can You Handle the Truth?*, could certainly change your life too.

Don has enjoyed more than 29 years of success as a real estate investor. He is both an optimist and a realist. He's learned all the pitfalls you might encounter, whether you plan to buy your first home or invest in real estate for profit. Success hasn't changed his passion for learning one bit, however. Even yet, he continues to educate himself in his profession, continuously seeking out new information, new guidelines, and new ways to help people succeed in real estate as he himself has done.

Do you want to create wealth and make all your real estate investment dreams come true? Do you long to buy your first home but something inside you is holding you back?

Don calls it a "fear of the unknown" and nothing more. The only cure for that, he insists, is education and knowledge. With almost three decades of real estate experience to his credit, Don is truly the qualified expert you need. In fact, I'd say the only thing that exceeds his know-how is his genuine passion for helping people.

When it's all said and done, not only can you can handle the truth, as told in *The Secret of Real Estate Revealed*, you need it if you want to make the right real estate choices for yourself and your family's future.

This book is not only easy to read and easy to understand, it is peppered throughout with Don's unique wit, wisdom and humor. He doesn't pull any punches and he seems to thrive on "telling it like it is," in his own unique, quirky style.

You will not only find this book delightfully entertaining but the ideas and information presented here will illuminate the inner workings of the real estate world for you once and for all.

Don knows the real estate business. His words ring loud and clear and I would suggest you or anyone you care about read this book before you even consider a mortgage or an investment property.

Don and I have a lot in common. His dad and my dad were brothers. That makes us first cousins. Neither one of our parents had a lot of money, but they instilled in us the importance of learning and helping others. And those rules have made both of us wealthy, happy and healthy. We passed this information along to our kids. Read the book and pass it along to yours.

Don often describes himself, quite jokingly, as a "guy who talks a lot."

People like myself who know him, either professionally or personally, will tell you we wouldn't have it any other way.

Perhaps he doesn't have to "remember anything" when he speaks, but what he says and writes about in this book is certainly – and most often – worth remembering.

—**Bob Proctor, bestselling author of *You Were Born Rich*
and featured in the hit movie *The Secret***

Acknowledgments

I would like to thank my parents, Howard and Katie Proctor, because without their positive influence, this would have never happened. Thank you to my grandmother, Christine MacGillivray Campbell, who was a writer signing CC at the end of all of her writing. CC was the only teacher at the one-room school known as the Welbeck School during the early 1900s. She always stressed the importance of good books and reading to my sisters and me during our youth. Thank you to my little sister, Jodi Ainsworth, who has always made my family's world brighter. Thanks to my favorite teachers, Mr. Scott Allgood, from the Simcoe Composite School; your intelligence is outshone by your humanity. Thank you to Dr. Tom Peters, PhD; your instruction in economics and your work ethic should be directed to our politicians. Thank you to my friend Bob Kowtaluk for educating me on the importance of added value, nobody ever taught me added value in school. Thank you to my friend Paul Arthur for intelligent sound advice and conversation. Thank you also to my legal counsel, Cornelius Brennan—a lawyer with a heart. I have been wonderfully instructed in life and in business by my dear Aunt Margaret Proctor Moir, and her one and only husband, Donald Moir. The gift of helping others has been reinvented with the Moir family. I must thank my secretaries, Jesse Masschaele and Meg LaPlante. Thanks also to the front-porch gang: Morgan Dale, Sarah, Jackie and Louise, the Huyges, Decker, Walsh, Nuno, Penner, the Davison Brothers, Jazmyne, Livingstone, Jesse, Bob, Chris, Josh, Joanne, Greenwood, and the Poppes. I want to thank the guys from primary maintenance, for whom I have the highest level of respect. The level of intelligence in that crew has not been equaled by any other group I have met.

To the working people of the world, this could never have been written without you.

IT'S NOT HAUNTED

Too many people are thinking of security instead of opportunity.
They seem to be more afraid of life than death.

—James F. Bymes

Remember that old, creepy house that you used to walk past in the neighborhood? You know the one—it had broken windows, it was missing siding, and the shutters were barely clinging to hope on one nail? The one that your friends double-dog dared you to go into? The one that everyone knew was haunted?

While that run-down shack might have given you and your friends some top-notch entertainment, in reality it was just an abandoned old house—a property in need of rehab, a flip waiting to happen. The emotions that you felt back then, and that many are feeling now in the housing market, are fear and outright panic. It doesn't have to be that way.

When you've been in the business of real estate as long as I have, you've just about seen it all. One of the things that still bothers me is the fear that I see in the eyes of potential homeowners, and it's not their fault. They want to be led by the hand to their dream home, but they are intimidated by what they don't know about the market and the professionals in it. Unfortunately, their fears are well founded, as many so-called professionals take advantage of both home buyers and sellers.

The reality of the market today is that you must keep your own best interests at heart while dealing with people who just want to make a sale. The real estate market is run mostly by realtors, and as commissioned salespeople, they have to sell houses to eat. Unfortunately, they will attempt to do that even if a potential sale is not in your best interest.

I know that there are many realtors out there who will argue with me that they only have their clients' best interests at heart and would never encourage them to agree to a deal that wasn't what the client wanted.

But believe me, this is not always the case. When that realtor's electricity is about to get cut off, he will do whatever he has to do and say whatever he has to say to get you to sign on the dotted line. If he doesn't, he won't be in business long. It has been my experience that the problem isn't with the home or the buyer or the seller. The problem lies with everyone else involved in the transaction who is trying to make a buck.

The purchase of a home is a big decision, and for many people, it is an emotional one. They picture themselves raising their family in the home, spending holidays together, and living out their lives in this place. This puts home buyers in a vulnerable position. They run the risk of falling in love with a home, and those emotions can overwhelm their sense of reason. The results can be disastrous if homeowners realize later that it wasn't the best home for them, or that they were encouraged to buy a larger home than they could really afford.

You might think that I am discouraging you from buying a home or investing in property, but actually the opposite is true. Real estate has proven to be a spectacular investment over the long haul, and I should know; I'm an investor myself. In fact, I'd recommend that you reject advice from any so-called real estate professional who isn't an investor and homeowner himself. Think about it; would you trust advice from an investment broker who didn't own any stocks? Of course not. Then why would you trust advice from a realtor who doesn't own property?

Before we get into dishing the dirt on how real estate transactions really work, we are going to talk about the fear factor that most people encounter when buying a home. A home is a very big purchase; it is most likely the biggest purchase that most people will ever make. Though there is a great deal of information out there to help buyers in today's market, I see people throwing money away each month on rent, when they could easily afford to own their own homes. They might as well light a match to that rent money and kiss it good-bye.

Even people who know that they can afford to buy a home often don't take that next step. They put if off, waiting for a better moment. Every moment is a good moment to buy real estate, if you know what you are doing and don't let the fear get the best of you. Let's examine a few of the most common concerns people have and dispel those fears once and for all.

1. The market is in a tailspin.

So what? In fact, the perfect time to buy real estate is when everyone else is selling. One of the most interesting truths about human beings is that fear can convince us that our dumbest moves are actually smart. We tell ourselves things such as, "I'm going to wait until the market recovers before I jump in," or "I'm putting my home on the market right now, so I don't lose any more money."

Like me, you've probably heard both of those statements repeatedly when the subject of real estate has come up at the office, on the golf course, or at the nail salon. If you've said them yourself, then you damn sure shouldn't ever admit it, or it will confirm to those you know that you don't understand the real estate market.

The whole idea of investments—and buying a home is an investment—is to buy low and sell high. You want to purchase the investment at a good price, hold it and allow it to appreciate, and then sell it at the maximum price the market will bear.

You must also realize that the market is very media- and emotion-driven, and the tendency to panic can get you in real trouble. We'll use Joe as an example.

Joe Bonehead sees on TV that homes are going into foreclosure at record rates. He doesn't realize that the media loves to dwell on negative hype. What they don't highlight is the fact that the interest rate is only a few percentage points above average. They make it sound like everyone Joe knows will soon be homeless, which is absolutely not true.

You may wonder, why would that good-looking anchorman or woman, who appears to be so trustworthy, mislead the listening public? Because that anchorperson works for a TV station that is a business and needs ratings. If the station can get you to tune in, it can sell more advertising at higher prices and make more money. Don't think that it is anything more glamorous or altruistic than that.

Let's get back to Joe. So, let's say he hears this report about foreclosures running rampant and believes it. Then he starts to worry that his home is losing its value, so he calls a realtor and has a chat about the market.

Now, the realtor is in the business of making transactions happen, not improving the market. Realtors make money when you buy, and they make money when you sell, regardless if the market is up or down. The realtor smells a listing and possible commission if he agrees with Joe that the value of his house might go down if he doesn't sell right now.

The next thing you know, Joe's house is sold for a fair price but at less than he wanted or could have gotten. He trusted the realtor's advice to take the offer, assuming it was the best he could do, when in reality, the realtor was going for a quick sale.

But guess what? Now Joe needs a place to live! So he must buy another house, and it's the realtor to the rescue (or buzzard to the carcass)! Joe must buy a house immediately in the same market he just sold into. He doesn't have time to make a truly rational decision or to wait for the right deal to come along. Joe trusts the realtor to show him the best house he can get for his money.

Remember, however, that the realtor lives on transactions, not whether Joe's new home is a good investment or not. Because of this, the realtor shows Joe a selection of homes to choose from, and Joe assumes that they are the best ones available. This may or may not be true.

More often, these are homes that the realtor feels that Joe will fall in love with and sign the papers on without a lot of hassle. The realtor makes the same money if he shows Joe one house or fifty, so the realtor will only show him a few and bet that Joe bites, so that the realtor doesn't have to put out more effort than is necessary to get his commission.

2. If I buy a house, I'll be cash poor.

One concept that many home buyers don't fully comprehend is the idea of trading up. You begin with a starter home, maybe a small one- or two-bedroom house. You then live in that house for about five years (which is the average length of time these days). Over those five years, you gain what is called equity. This is the difference between what the house is worth and what you owe on it. If you've ever looked at a mortgage schedule that shows how much will be left on your loan after each payment, you realize that you don't really start whittling away at that debt until about year ten (for a thirty-year mortgage). This is because you are paying more interest in the early years.

What many people don't take into account is that while you might feel like you are paying your mortgage and getting nowhere, your home is escalating in value each year. This escalation means that the gap between the value of the property and what you owe widens, even though you don't make a great deal of headway on the mortgage itself. This gap (equity) is your best friend. When you decide to get a larger home, this equity is converted to cash when you sell and can be applied to the down payment on the next property. As you move up to larger and more valuable homes, this appreciation escalates, and you need less actual cash (if any at all) to move up to a more expensive home.

One common error that I see home buyers make is that they try to score the big house right off the bat. Talk about being strapped for cash! It sucks to buy a castle and then have to live in the dark because you can't afford the electric bill. So it's important to take a little time and let equity work in your favor.

Another error I often see made is what I call "house hopping." These people buy and sell houses constantly—every two years or so—which means that any gains are eaten up by transaction fees and closing costs. In essence, they are still in a renting frame of mind and are not growing their wealth.

It's easy to feel like you have plunged into a deep vat of debt right after you buy a home. However, you have to realize that while you are responsible for the payments, you actually had a very small outlay of cash, if any at all, if you used your equity from a previous home. Meanwhile, that new home is gaining equity every minute. Even while you sleep, your house is making you money. Mortgages are one of the best money-making inventions ever because they allow you to make this money (equity) through the use of someone else's cash. The mortgage company forked over almost all of the dough, yet you get the equity! How great is that?

3. The "C" word.

Commitment can be a fabulous thing because it gives you roots and a certain comfort level that what you have is yours, and not just a temporary lifestyle. However, the idea of committing to a thirty- or even fifteen-year note can scare the life right out of some people. I regularly tell those who are a little skittish that if they don't plan to stay in one location for more than three years, then buying a home isn't right for their situation.

While some people like to be free of long-term financial entanglements, most people eventually settle down and want to stay in one place for a while. However, the idea that you're stuck with a property for thirty years isn't reality anymore. It is an investment, which means that you can sell it at any time.

People can really get hung up on this idea of commitment if they allow themselves to. But it's important to remember that nothing is forever. If you decide after only a few years that the location or house isn't right for you, you can always get a new one.

4. A house is constant work.

I know people who have not bought a house because they perceive that it will bring a great deal of additional work into their lives. I can only guess that they've seen one too many home improvement shows. It is up to you what type of house you buy, and if you aren't a maintenance expert or a fixer-upper type of person, then there is still a house or condo for you.

I have to wonder why people are so afraid of changing a light bulb. Did they stick a paperclip into a light socket as a child or have an emotional breakdown trying to start the lawnmower? Oh wait, I know—it's work.

For some reason, there are those out there who do not want to put any effort into their homes, and really, that's fine. You can pay people to do the work for you, or you can buy a house that is virtually maintenance free. But why would you refuse to invest because of it? If this investment makes you money while you sleep, then I'd say that's a pretty cool thing and should be uniquely attractive to someone who is allergic to work.

Whether you want a yard or just a balcony overlooking the city, there is a home suitable for you that will allow you to take advantage of the real estate market.

5. I'm scared.

Now we're getting to the root of the problem. All of the issues and excuses I hear from people concerning real estate purchasing and investing basically boil down to fear. If the idea of getting a thirty-year mortgage for several hundred thousand dollars strikes fear into your heart, then no house will convince you otherwise.

Realize that fear is an emotional reaction, and if you can learn to overcome your emotions and educate yourself, then you will have a much higher comfort level and confidence in your own decision-making ability.

And remember, even if you make a less-than-stellar choice, it is still fixable. You are not committed for life. You can get always get out of it or come up with creative solutions to mitigate the issues. One advantage you have over everyone else is that I'm here to guide you and teach you to spot the deals— and the snakes—within the real estate world.

Chapter 1

REVIEW

- Keep your own best interests at heart when buying a home.

- Emotions put the home buyer in a vulnerable position.

- Every moment is a good moment to buy the right house.

- Don't let market swings make you irrational.

- Think long-term wealth, not short-term gain.

- Don't let fear kill a good deal.

STICKS AND STONES, BABY!

Great minds have purposes; little minds have wishes. Little minds are subdued by misfortunes; great minds rise above them.

—Washington Irving

It can be very difficult to separate the emotional attachment you have for your home from the financial investment. We raise families, create memories, and live our lives within the walls. But the reality is that any house is just sticks and stones—that's it.

The emotions that people invest in their homes range from warm, fuzzy feelings to downright ridiculous. I've even met those who name their homes as if they have personalities. You don't ever hear an investor of stocks say, "That's right; I have five hundred shares of IBM. I call them Bob."

The problem is that we perceive that our home is part of our identity, and that it says something distinct about who we are and what we are. But just like pegging your identity to the type of car you drive, this is misplaced emotion, and because a home is the biggest investment that most people ever make, it can cost you a bundle.

Another mistake that some people make when the real estate market swings wildly, is they go from an emotional attachment to their house to fear for their financial lives. This sudden shift to investor from home lover can warp your perspective and cause you to consider some not only irrational, but financially devastating actions.

IT'S ALL ABOUT RESALE

You buy your home to live in for a long time, right? Wrong. Depending on where you live, the averages show that you will be putting that home on the market again in anywhere from four to eight years. That's pretty short term for real estate, but it shows the way we live these days. It is extremely rare for anyone to stay with the same employer for thirty years, and it's just as rare for someone to stay in the same house.

In part, this is due to our finances. A young couple or a single person just starting out only has so much money and generally buys a very modest house. These young people also have specific needs. Small homes or condos with no yards are popular with these folks, as they tend not to have children. Remember those days? When you didn't notice the peeling paint, dripping faucets, and creaking rafters because you were so thrilled to have a place of your own?

Eventually, the time comes to move up. Either you get married or get a better job, or you just get tired of the mice running rampant through your house like pets. Now you have to sell that home that seemed so perfect just a short time ago. You wonder who you're ever going to get to pay money for this dump.

Now you are being a little more objective about the resale of your investment. The time to think about resale is when you are buying. There are things you cannot control about the real estate market. What you can control is the type and condition of home that you buy to guarantee the best resale possible, no matter what market conditions exist when it comes time to sell.

You hear all the time that the most vital attribute to consider when buying real estate is location. The type of neighborhood and surrounding area can have a tremendous effect on the value of and demand for your home a few years from now. For example, purchasing a small fixer-upper in a great neighborhood can be a great way to maximize your budget when you are young. Conversely, buying a little nicer home in a declining area can really hurt you, as a few years from now it can be a downright ghetto, and buyers will be few and far between.

Once you get past that initial starter property, there are a few more items to take into consideration:

- Don't buy the most expensive or the least expensive home in a particular neighborhood. If the home you are considering doesn't match the quality of surrounding homes, you'll have a rough time getting a good price when you sell.

- If the home you're interested in is the only nice one in the area, the surrounding homes may tend to drag down its value when it comes time to have it appraised.

- Be one of the first buyers in a new development. The last buyers to purchase a home in a new development generally will pay more. By the time the last residents have moved in, the original buyers have made a quick profit on their investment.

- Be sure your home is near major employers and transportation. Quick access to employment centers and major highways or transport are even more important as gas prices escalate. Use this in your favor.

- Watch out for noise. Don't buy a home on a busy street or one that backs up to a busy street. Instead, look for those on dead-end streets or cul-de-sacs that are a few blocks away from all the hubbub. Also avoid houses close to trains and airport flyways. It is very important to ask about noise when you are looking, as realtors tend to schedule appointments and open houses at quiet times if they know noise is an issue.

- Do look for an area with a good school system and nearby churches and synagogues. These might be very important factors for a potential buyer at resale time. If you are buying a small home, areas near universities can be ideal, as they will always have plenty of ready buyers.

- Check out the local planning commission and see what new developments and shopping centers are planned. Buying near a planned site will escalate in value in a few years when the projects are complete.

- Look for items within your home that are unique from your neighbors' and might make your property more desirable. These might include a corner lot, a larger back yard, a double-car garage instead of a single, a patio or deck, and upgraded baths and kitchen.

All this sounds pretty easy, and it is. But what about when you sell? It's no secret that most peoples' homes never look better than when they get ready to sell. All those little things that you let go and live with while you're making the payments just won't do when you're trying to maximize your investment.

The trick is to think "investment" and not "designer central." You have to focus on what gives your buyer the most value, not what you personally like, and it doesn't have to cost big bucks to make a big difference.

1. Kitchens are money in the bank. Most families just about live in the kitchen; it's the center of the home. An outdated kitchen can be a deal breaker. For just a little bit of money, you can make some cosmetic changes that give the impression that your tired, old kitchen is newer than it really is. Little things like a new faucet, new cabinet hardware, and a fresh coat of paint can make a big difference. Updating old light fixtures can do wonders as well. If your budget is a little larger, perhaps new countertops or flooring might be strong selling points.

2. Give appliances a facelift. If your kitchen appliances don't match, order new doors or face panels for them. If they are in reasonably good condition, the fact that they match can make all the difference. I can't tell you what it's like to take people into a kitchen with white, almond, and avocado green appliances. First impressions are so important. You can either have people get the impression that the kitchen is cohesive and ready to go, or they will assume that everything needs to be replaced, which will affect their offer.

3. Baths are the bomb! Next to the kitchen, bathrooms are the most important rooms to update. The good news is that a little cash goes a long way here as well. Little things such as replacing the toilet seat and light fixtures can make a big difference. If you have one of those 1950s pink toilets, then for less than $100 you can get a nice white one and make the seller think you've stepped into this century. Add a new shower curtain and matching rugs, and it looks great. Don't forget the floor. In some cases, you may not even need to remove the old flooring. You might be able to just lay new vinyl over the top. Even if you have to replace the flooring entirely, bathrooms have such small square footage that it's not usually a budget buster.

Many people don't realize that tubs and tile can be resurfaced for a very low cost. You don't have to replace everything, and if your tub and sinks are basically in good shape, you can quickly and easily make them look brand new.

4. Add a bedroom. If you have a house that has a den or an office or just one of those weird rooms you can't really categorize, there's no reason that it can't be made into a bedroom. Additional bedrooms enhance the value of your house because potential buyers can live in the house longer as their families expand. It also opens your house to an additional category of buyers who need more room. Even if it takes a few studs and some drywall to accomplish the deed, it can be very low cost for the value it adds.

5. Pay attention to what works. By this, I mean fix all of the flaws that you've just lived with all of these years. It's often very worthwhile to hire an electrician and plumber for a couple of hours to look over your electrical services, wrap or fix loose wires, fix any faulty outlets, and check for and fix any water leaks. Those details tell a buyer that someone has really taken care of the home, and they won't need a handyman the second they walk in the door.

6. It smells like a wet dog. Few people realize how dirty their carpet is. Unclean carpets can be the main contributor to a musty odor in a home. Years of tracking snow and mud across a carpet really can do some damage as well. New carpeting can instantly make a home look clean and updated and smell better. A professional carpet cleaning is an inexpensive investment, especially if your rugs are in good shape and are neutral colors. If it really isn't in the budget for new carpet, some well-placed area rugs can at least hide some of the worst flaws.

7. Light makes everything look better. If you have big, heavy drapes on your windows, consider getting lighter ones and pulling them back, so full, natural light enters your home. Light makes a room look inviting and larger. If you have a dark room or basement, adding more lighting can help give the idea of light in what might be a dark and off-putting area. Home stores offer a wide range of inexpensive and nice-looking ceiling fixtures these days. If you have a ceiling fan and light, you can also buy replacement fan blades (leaving the fan body in place) to update the fixture's look.

8. Reframe your entry. Do you have a flimsy little knob on your main entry door? If so, spring for a substantial-looking handle-and-lock set and even a brass kick plate. You can also paint the front door a different color than the house to make it stand out more. House numbers that are brass or stainless steel can enhance the look of the entry area as well.

9. Update the curb appeal. Although it sounds like basic common sense, a nicely mowed lawn, a few well-placed shrubs, and a swept walkway make a great first impression. When buyers drive by your home, you want them to take notice and really look twice. While a Chevy up on blocks may make them look twice, don't expect any offers. If you don't have a green thumb, consider hiring a landscaper to install some new sod, plant a few evergreen shrubs, and give your front yard a good cleanup. Perception is everything, and your home has to look good to command a good price.

SO IF IT'S SO EASY . . .

People ask me all the time, "If it's so easy, why do so many people blow it?" As much as I'd like to say that there are circumstances that can't be avoided, most of the time that isn't true. The problem is that when dollars are involved, our emotions take over, and our common sense goes out the window.

Let's look at the story of Glen and Glenda Greed. They put their house on the market for $173,000. Their house payment is $1,300 per month, and they owe $130,000 on the mortgage. Two weeks later, they get an offer for $165,000. They consider it but turn it down because they are convinced that another buyer will want to pay more. Six months later, they accept an offer for $169,000. They won, right? They did get someone to pay more, but let's look at the real cost.

Over six months, they paid $7,800 in payments that added hardly anything to their equity, as they are still paying mostly interest. This means that while they made an additional $4,000 by waiting for a better offer, the wait time (six months) cost them $7,800. This means that they actually lost $3,800 on the transaction. Had they taken a lower offer within two weeks, they would have come out just as well and could have moved on and not had people traipsing through their house for six months.

I've seen examples that were much worse. Some people end up with homes on the market for more than a year because they don't realize that time costs them money—and it doesn't guarantee them a higher offer.

One of the hardest things for homeowners to overcome is their own expectations. The brain processes expectations in a much more intense way than it processes the actual experience. So, the hope of making money often feels better than actually making the money does, and the fear of losing money often feels worse than actually losing the money. So the Greed family felt better about their higher offer than the lower one because it was closer to their expectations, even though it actually cost them money.

You may have noticed that when it comes to money, people are not always logical. The human brain developed to solve the very simple problems of finding food and shelter, courting mates, and avoiding danger, and our ancestors had to make simple calculations about risk and reward, all in the absence of money. In the modern world, almost every risk and reward that a human being faces is either symbolized or mediated by money. Money is not a reward in itself, but there are very few rewards you can get where you don't need money. Money taps into the most ancient and powerful emotions that the human brain can experience. Many people feel that they are thinking and deliberating about financial decisions, but what they often don't realize is they are really deciding with their emotions.

The excitement that you feel from thinking you are going to make money is very intense. You pin your hopes and dreams on that, even though the market may not bear out your asking price. The only way to keep yourself from falling into the pit of emotional decision making is to evaluate all the information. Think through different scenarios and talk with your family about how you will handle them. What if someone offers five thousand less, or ten, or even twenty? How will you respond? How long will you leave the house on the market before you reevaluate your price?

This doesn't mean that you should stack it up against the experience of your buddy at work or your Uncle Joe. Your home is unique, and the market conditions are always changing. Don't allow yourself to react emotionally and therefore cheat yourself out of the best home or best price possible.

REVIEW

- Don't become too emotionally attached to a home.

- Think about the resale value before you buy.

- As in investor, think about what people need the most and find homes that fit that need.

- Kitchens and bathrooms allow the most bang for the buck when fixing up a home.

- Curb appeal can't be taken for granted and adds to a home's value.

- Understand what price the market will bear for your home, not what you think it should be worth.

STOP WANTING—START EARNING

The important thing is this: To be able at any moment to sacrifice what we are for what we could become.

—Charles Dubois

I hear people say all the time, "I want to be debt free," or "I want a house," or "I want a car," and all that reverberates in my mind are the words, "I want, I want, I want." I will say that if you want to be debt free, you can be. If you want material things, you can have them, too, but neither is possible if you do not make a plan to make it happen. What plan do you have to acquire the things that you want, or do you even have one? You'd be surprised how little time people spend on this aspect of creating wealth.

People also sit around and gripe about how much things cost and how high prices are. Even if they are on a plan to pay down their debt and improve their situation, they still complain as if it's someone else's fault that they are in this situation. They feel that they are suffering when they are really gaining their own freedom. There has to be a balance between wanting and spending, and we should not have to continue this circular pattern of impulsive spending to satisfy a want that can never be satisfied.

Many people's actions are triggered by the emotion of wanting what they see. However, philosophers tell us that we see things with our mind's eye, and we take a mental picture of what we want and begin thinking about getting those things. This can easily turn into an obsession or a wishing game if people lack the resources to obtain items and then lean heavily on credit to buy them.

Obviously some peoples' eyes have become larger than their pocketbooks. When people fail to properly plan to obtain the things that they want and use credit to obtain them, before long they might find themselves in deep debt. The short-term satisfaction is outweighed by the regret they feel after the purchase, which they can no longer enjoy because they have the fear of losing it. These actions may be attributed to the mismanagement of money or just plain poor decision making.

I wish I had enough money to pay for that house, boat, or plane, they may say to themselves. This might be the case for some, but for others who are struggling just to keep up with their current bills and necessities, it is an unfortunate time, due to the economical crisis we are experiencing today. Increased costs and unforeseen business failures may strip away what extra money was flowing in.

Nonetheless, there is hope. To come up out of either situation will take a confident and positive attitude and a desire to analyze the situation to make a determination for change. First, there must be a conscious decision to stop creating more debt that isn't helping you. This isn't to say that all debt is bad, and of course, a mortgage is debt. But a mortgage helps you to buy an asset that gains in value rather than depreciates. Credit card debt and loans that allow you to buy things that depreciate are not good. This is because the minute you purchase them, their value goes down.

One of the first steps to getting off this bad-debt roller coaster is to figure out where you stand. The following is a generic expense chart that you can use to write down your expenses. This is important because you need to see where your money is going.

Anytime you think about expenses, you must avoid the common pitfall of "guesstimating" your expenses. Most people overestimate their income and underestimate their expenses. Always write down your actual income and expenses using check stubs, statements, and online account information. Accuracy in this initial step will make it much easier to develop a realistic wealth plan.

Month

Category	Monthly Budget	Monthly Actual	Difference	Comments
Income				
Monthly pay (after taxes)				
Alimony or child support received				
Other income				
Total Monthly Income				
Expenses: Housing				
Mortgage or rent				
Real estate property tax				
Personal property tax				

Category	Monthly Budget	Monthly Actual	Difference	Comments
Homeowner's or renter's insurance				
Homeowners association or condo fees				
Total Housing Expenses				
Expenses: Utilities				
Electric				
Gas/heating oil				
Water/sewage				
Telephone				
Trash collection				
Cable TV				
Internet provider				
Cell phone				
Total Utilities Expense				
Expenses: Transportation				

Car payments				
Car Insurance				
Car maintenance/repair*				
Mass transit costs				
Gas				
Parking/tolls				
Tags/inspection*				
Total Transportation Expenses				
Loans/credit				
Credit cards				
Child support				
Entertainment				
Miscellaneous				
Total Credit Expenses				
Total Monthly Income				
Total Monthly Expenses				
Difference				

When you earn, you set the tone for what you desire, not what you want. You create ways to pay for expensive purchases rather than borrowing to buy things. If you have to borrow, you should create a solid repayment plan as a security precaution.

Companies are always thinking of creative ways to market and sell products to you. Colors, designs, lighting, tone, and elegance are all tactics geared toward your emotions. Salespeople know what to throw at you to get you to make purchases. That's why they call it a pitch. When the sales pitch is right, and you are in a state of wanting, you look like the puppy that is salivating for its kibbles and bits, and they know how to get your money!

Earning is something that cannot be measured in terms of money alone. Earning is so much more than that. Earning is also learning. For example, learning how to control your emotions increases your earning potential.

Let's say that you saw something that you wanted, for example, a $30,000 Limited Edition Harley. Instead of paying cash now or buying it on credit, you decide to wait an additional two years and earn enough to pay cash for the motorcycle. You also make the decision that you will put the extra money you earn into an investment with an interest rate of 8 percent. You create another source of income and are able to save $22,000 over two years. By this time, that same Harley has depreciated to $24,000, and is much more affordable. Your investment has matured, so you've earned an additional $2,200 in interest. So if you make the purchase after two years, you've just saved yourself $8,200 and accumulated no additional debt. This is the best method for getting what you want without going broke.

EVERYTHING COSTS

Understand that everything you acquire costs money. People don't want to face the reality that everything has a cost. Most people want something for nothing, but businesses are designed to make profits, to create jobs, and boost the economy, and it can't be done if they are giving everything away for free. Money has to circulate! Nonetheless, you can choose to spend differently. Become an investor, purchase income-generating assets instead of depreciating assets, plan initially to limit debt, and eventually seek to become debt free.

There is a hidden force working behind the scenes in all of our financial transactions. It is discussed daily on the financial media. It is spelled out when we purchase homes. It has been communicated and used as a bargaining tool by everyone from the most sophisticated investor to the local "Joe the Plumber." It is called compound interest, and it can work for you or against you.

Compound interest works for investors because it means that you earn interest on both principle and interest. So if you invest $10,000 and you are getting 5 percent interest, then at the end of the first year, you will have $10,500. Now in the second year, you earn interest on the full $10,500, and therefore earn $525. Compound interest allows you to accumulate and earn more money faster.

Unfortunately, if you are in debt, compound interest works against you, costing you more money the longer you stay in debt.

By understanding the difference in interest rates, you can save literally thousands of dollars. If you purchase a home for $177,000 with an 8 percent interest rate, you can have a monthly payment of $1,300 per month. You might think that this is a good deal, but if you do what it takes to lower your interest rate to 6 percent, your payment lowers to $1,060 per month, and that will save you an average of $2,880 dollars per year. This equates to a total savings of $85,500 dollars over the life of a thirty-year loan. This is one way to free up money to invest in other sources of income.

Buying a home is the biggest investment most people will make, so it really pays to understand how to get that home for the best price and interest rate possible, and then to use that extra money to invest in other properties or investment products. If you are in debt in other areas such as credit cards, this extra cash can be used to dig out of that hole and start you on the path to financial freedom.

I have heard many people gripe and complain about some credit card companies and how they are charging incredible interest rates and taking advantage of them. Why blame the company for setting the high rates, when you're in no position to negotiate because of bad credit history, previous poor financial decisions, and little knowledge of how it all works? Furthermore, lenders do not force you to put items on credit cards, take out loans, or borrow money; they leave the decision all up to you! Most companies simply offer an avenue for you to get what you want today without having to wait to earn the money. Of course, this lifestyle is expensive and will cost you tremendously in the long run.

The amount on the credit card bill that you must pay each month seems to be a very small amount when you are only making the minimum payments. The payment submitted is eaten up by what's owed in interest first, and then what is left is applied to principle, leaving you with an increased balance, rather than a decreased balance, over time.

It's important to increase your awareness to the potential pitfalls of owning items and take on the responsibility so that you're financially and mentally prepared.

THE VALUE OF MENTORS

It is important to know that if you feel as if you are in over your head right now, there is help available to you. You aren't the first to feel overwhelmed or concerned that you are on the brink of financial trouble. Even if you are meeting your obligations, that nagging feeling that you aren't getting ahead as quickly as you'd like tells you that there's more. We can't do everything alone, and finding a mentor can shorten your learning curve.

I will insert a note of caution here. Not all mentors have your best interests at heart. There are numerous gurus who will encourage you to sign up for their program or buy their system. This is not mentoring, it's a sales pitch. While experts in the field of finance can be useful, just be aware of what you're getting, and don't rely on anyone else to make the ultimate decision with your finances.

The ultimate financial lesson for most people is the understanding that they must practice self-control. You must focus on what you really want for your life and stop making impulse decisions that affect you negatively. Do you really need those new shoes and party dress that you put on your credit card at 20 percent interest, or do you want to save for a down payment on your first investment property? Do you want to play an extra four rounds of golf this week, or would you rather start an Internet business that will start making you money? These are the daily decisions we all make that determine our future wealth.

Success is not measured by the amount of money you have in the bank; it is determined by your sense of accomplishment. When you create a plan and take control of your financial well being, you start on the path to that sense of accomplishment. Practice patience and control the want.

"PARETO" YOUR WAY TO WEALTH

In the 1800s, an Italian economist, Vilfredo Pareto, coined the phrase the Pareto Principle. The basic idea is that 20 percent of your effort produces 80 percent of your results. How does this rule apply to gaining control over your finances?

There are several ways this idea applies to your finances. The first is on the side of cutting expenses. Look at what you spend your money on, and immediately cut 10 percent. You may think that you're stretched thin already, but it's the old balance between want and need. You should easily find 10 percent of your expenses that you could do without. Now go back through the numbers and cut another 10 percent. This is more challenging, but it is worth doing because it now frees up 20 percent of your income that could go to reducing debt or building investments. Just refinancing some of your current debt at better interest rates could do wonders for your monthly cash flow.

The important concept to remember is that you must look at each aspect of your financial life and see if there are options you aren't investigating that could help you either create more income, or move things around to produce more cash flow for investing.

HOME REFINANCING

It used to be that you could borrow money with interest-only options or an adjustable-rate mortgage. Low payments could be made in the first few years and the loans refinanced after two years before the interest rate would adjust to the current market rate. However, since the housing market crisis, the value of the home may be lower than the original purchase price, and therefore you may not be able to refinance. In a refinance deal, lenders will usually only lend up to 80 percent of the loan (loan-to-value), and therefore you may be stuck with the current loan.

In situations where loan payments would double for some homeowners, the refinance option was a method to avoid foreclosure and save the home; however, it may not be an option now. If you find yourself in this predicament, the best avenue is to immediately contact the lender and see what options they offer. Lenders don't want to foreclose if another solution can be found, but you can't wait until you are behind on payments to approach them, or your options will be far fewer.

KEEP THE CASH

You make your money when you purchase a home, not when you sell it. Home ownership means many things to many people, but most would agree that it represents a certain amount of security and hope for the future. It says that you have accomplished something that not everyone has, but that most people would like to. While it is a great achievement, it can also play on your emotions.

We have all sat in front of the TV recently, listening to the declining economic indicators and predictions of how we are sliding further into a recession. Has this ever made you turn to your spouse and say, "I can't understand why there are so many foreclosures. Do you think that this will affect our home value?"

Even if you have no intention of selling your home right now, understand that most people buy homes as an investment, and when the investment value is threatened, they become emotional and develop an anxiety that creates fear. The home generates equity and provides a dwelling for your family. But if the home is your only investment, then you may be in trouble. Let's take a look at this concept in greater detail.

Although buying a home is good, you should never put all your investment eggs in one basket. Land will most likely appreciate in value over time, but this might happen slowly, and if you do not seek to sell your home anytime soon, then think of it as a long-term investment. The money put into the home will build equity eventually, but the downside is that if you ever need to use the money, you will have to borrow it. This is associated with taking out an equity loan, again with interest, that you'll have to pay back. You will have to determine what works for you, but if this is your only investment, learn now how to diversify your portfolio.

It is important to never rely on home equity loans. As we have seen with the current financial crisis, the rules could change at any time, and what is an option today might not be an option tomorrow.

Today the job market is so sporadic that lay-offs and company failures are imminent. By tying up all of your available cash into your home, you lock away the opportunity to access it quickly. Again, having a well-thought-out plan as to why and how you will own your home or investment property is the key. By not diversifying into other income-generating assets, you may be unable to keep up with the demand for your mortgage due to unforeseen circumstances.

If you do decide to refinance, you will find that you may receive a lower interest rate, but you increase the life of the loan, and you'll pay closing costs all over again. If there are ways to restructure the amortization schedule with the lender and not refinance, this may be a good option for you. The important idea is to be creative and to get help as soon as there is trouble in the air, not when the wolf is already at the door.

FINDING OTHER WAYS TO SAVE MONEY

Carol and her husband live in Virginia and decided to purchase a larger home for their growing family. They had good credit and understood how interest works. But Carol was creative in finding additional money to save when buying her house. She negotiated the price of the home and asked the seller to pay up to $10,000 in closing costs. Actual closing costs were around $6,500, and Carol used the additional $3,500 to pay down the points on the loan with the lender, lowering her interest rate. This means that her monthly payments are lower, and she will save literally tens of thousands of dollars over the life of the loan.

BEGIN AT THE BEGINNING

When preparing to reach your financial goals, the following suggestions will help you get off to a great start.

Step One—Be objective

- Gather all bills and evaluate them to determine what you owe and what your payment habits are.

- If you pay your bills late, seek ways to pay your debt on time, such as automating payments. This will help raise your credit score and put you in better standing with the companies you owe.

- Remember taxes! Don't stop paying what is due to the government to try to get ahead. One of the worst debts you can have is a tax debt, as it affects many other aspects of your life.

- It is necessary that you pay yourself first and have an emergency fund; however, this cannot be done if you are a free spender. If you are purchasing unnecessarily out of habit or to socialize, stop it! Stop it right now! Eliminate these unhealthy habits and get control of your finances.

- Find ways to save on utilities, either by seeking out alternate providers or by evaluating your usage. Do the same with your car. Evaluate your driving habits to see if there are options for commuting or carpooling.

- Control the urge to splurge on expensive clothing, shoes, foods, entertainment, and other material items. You must commit to limiting your accumulation of debt before you can reduce it.

- Track your progress. No matter what your goal, if you can see how far you've come, it offers encouragement to keep going.

Step Two—Prioritize

- Prioritize your bills that are considered necessities and commit to making these payments on time. This means that you first pay your house payment and utilities even before you buy food. If you have to eat beans and rice for a short time, then do so. Making excuses and complaining won't help. You created the mess; you have to clean it up. Allowing bills to accumulate causes emotional distress, and it's hard to think clearly under these conditions. It is vital for you to have a clear mind to be able to create ideas and solutions. This cannot be done if you are consumed by worry about whether your lights or water will be turned off for non-payment.

- Identify how many credit cards are in the household. In the event that you discover that there are too many cards, you may want to refer to a Consumer Credit Counseling Agency to assist you with prioritizing and paying your bills. CCCs can consolidate bills so that you have one payment. You make your payment to them, and they will in turn disburse the money. Creditors are more likely to work with you if you are getting assistance from a reputable credit agency. If you hit hard times, the credit card companies might offer you a delayed payment plan as long as you work with the credit counseling agency. There are pros and cons associated with this type of endeavor, so you should do the research and determine what's best for you.

- Remember that good credit helps lenders associate with you. Credit is the bond between you and the lender that establishes trust. This trust is a key component to eventual financial independence.

MANAGING EMOTIONS

It's hard to watch property values around you fall and not be concerned. In some areas, the values have fallen 20 percent or more. For example, if your home was purchased for $180,000, and due to market declines, the value went down to $160,000, how would that make you feel? It appears that this is a bad thing. A $20,000 decrease is a lot of money, but remember that it is only on paper. This is not money you plan to touch anytime soon; therefore, do not let it affect you if you plan to continuing living in your home at least another two years. The market can change tremendously by then.

When the value decreases, something else happens in your favor. You pay less money in annual taxes. Also, if you are a property investor, you might find opportunities to acquire more properties at a discount that will benefit you in the long run. Opportunity often comes disguised as a recession.

Chapter 3

REVIEW

- You must have a plan.
- Stop creating new debt.
- Know your actual expenses.
- Money has to circulate.
- Understand how interest works, and pay attention to your rate.
- You have the answer within you.

Chapter 4

LOOK FOR RUBIES, NOT DIAMONDS

What we see depends mainly on what we look for.

—John Lubbock

When you are looking for a home, either your first or an upgrade from your current one, there are some rules of thumb and cautionary tales to consider. Depending on your needs and wants, the kind of house you look for is really up to you. Do you want that family home with a pool and large backyard? Or maybe you're looking for that open floor plan with an outdoor fireplace and built-in bar for entertaining? The one thing to always keep in mind is the resale value, so you don't want a home that starts out with some significant issues.

We already talked a bit about how important location is. I know of a particular development that has beautiful homes, most on cul-de-sacs with gardens and walking paths. It's really a beautiful place, and it's close to great schools and major shopping areas. Sounds great, right?

Looks can be deceiving. This particular development is built on a 100-year flood plain. That means that it is completely flooded on average once every hundred years. No big deal, you say, a hundred years is a long time. Well, much like the guy who puts his quarter in the slot machine and hits a jackpot, there's no way to know if you have a hundred years, or one year, or one week before the next flood. So don't get too excited until you check out all the facts.

Likewise, purchasing a home on a beach sounds great, but you need to check the hurricane frequency. I know some Texans who not only lost their beach homes in Galveston during Hurricane Ike, they also lost their beach! There's not even a place to rebuild if they wanted to, and insurance doesn't pay for losing your land, just for the structure. You have to watch out for the fine print that you don't read when you're buying the house.

These types of issues highlight the importance of thinking of your home as an investment first and a playground second.

One of the best ways for many people to maximize their financial gain on a home is to buy one that needs some work. Now, before you roll your eyes, just think about it rationally. You don't have to buy the money-pit house that is in need of a full rehab. You should consider one that needs some updating or some cosmetic fixes, and that is basically sound otherwise. This type of house can be purchased less expensively than other homes in a particular area and will escalate much faster in value once the work is done.

While your home must meet your needs, you should not make alterations that will devalue the house. Knocking down a wall between two bedrooms to make a den is a bad idea, as buyers value the additional bedroom much more. Likewise, you shouldn't remove an extra bath or reduce the size of the kitchen, even if you don't cook. The next buyer might want a larger kitchen, and it could make a big difference in the price you get.

Your home will most likely be one of the largest purchases of your lifetime. It's especially important not to buy too quickly or because you are eager to get into a home. Defining what exactly you're looking for in a home can be time –consuming, but it will save you time, energy, and money in the long run.

Before you start looking at homes, sit down and make a list of the characteristics you're looking for in a home, ranked from most to least important. Keep those priorities in mind as you look at homes, and update the list based on the homes you tour.

Important considerations include everything from affordability to ample closet space, the style of home (rambler, split-level, colonial), size and location of property, proximity to highways or transportation, and home condition (fixer-upper, move-in ready). Now take this list and prioritize it. What is your number-one priority? Realize that few homes will be an exact fit, and it may become a process of compromise on the less important issues.

Plan to look at numerous homes before making the decision to buy. Many people carry along a digital camera so they can keep track of which home had what features. Take good notes on the homes you tour, and keep track of how they rank on your list of must-haves. Don't rule out a home, sight unseen, because it doesn't have a swimming pool or hardwood floors; you can always make cosmetic changes once you've moved in. The most important items to look for are the ones you can't easily change—the surrounding area, the school district, and your neighbors.

If you go along, month after month, rejecting every home that you see, then it's time to reevaluate your list. Are you expecting too much in your price range? Are some of your wants unrealistic? For example, if you are expecting granite countertops and a pool in a two-bedroom, one-bathroom home, you don't understand the housing market—at all. I often see this with young couples, especially if their parents are well off. They want to replicate that lifestyle, but they don't have the bankroll to support it, and often they end up buying way more house than they can afford.

Of course, young people aren't the only ones who get into this mess. Most people want to live in a nice house in a nice neighborhood, but how nice depends on how big a mortgage you are willing to have. You note that I said willing. Just because a bank approves you for a certain amount, that doesn't mean that you should max it out. You have to remember than moving up to a larger house also means a move up in utilities and other expenses. This can really add up to the point that you struggle each month just to make your payments. The emotional trauma and stress often cause sleepless nights and family squabbles, and no house is worth that.

THE MONEY PIT

The whole idea of this chapter is to encourage you to search for rubies instead of diamonds when looking for a home. This means that you know exactly which flaws can be ignored and which ones will cost you big. Generally, the things that will cost you the most aren't necessarily obvious to the naked eye, but there are some clues.

Let's look at some of the biggest offenders:

- Foundation—If the potential house is a replica of the Leaning Tower of Pisa, have some pasta, but don't buy that house. If there are cracks in the foundation, just don't go there. Also, if the floor of the living room resembles the rolling hills of California, it's probably not a good bet, either. Even if the floor seems somewhat even (contractors are great illusionists), large cracks at the corners of doors and windows will give you a clue that all is not right underneath the house. Most sellers will tell you that the house has just settled, but you don't want one that is settling to China.

- The view—we all want a home that has a great view, but some are better than others. For example, is the neighbor's bedroom window mere feet from your living room window? If so, then entertainment could take on a whole new meaning for your family. Look up and down the street. Are things neat and tidy, or are trailers and old cars sitting everywhere? What about the back yard? Are there bottles of Colt 45 or trash laying outside the fence? Details such as these give you an indication of the quality of life you might have if you moved in.

- Plumbing—this will require a qualified inspector to assess, and that is not your Uncle Earl. Many plumbing jobs on homes are do-it-yourself specials and can result in lakes of raw sewage, poor water flow, and general misery for the home's occupants. Also, just because there is a faucet, that doesn't mean it works, so every fixture should be tested by the inspector. I've often seen newbies look at a home and start talking about moving things around in a bathroom. Remodeling is fine, and as I've said, it is a great way to increase a home's value. But toilets and tubs aren't decorator items, and moving them around in a bathroom can incur significant plumbing expense.

- Electrical—while often unseen, crappy electrical work can do more damage to your pocketbook than you realize. Circuit breakers are nothing to mess with, so here again, an expert can give you the real story. There are some clues that the electrical wiring in the home can be questionable, especially if it is an older home that has had additions. Do lights flicker when the heating or air conditioning flip on? Are there switches that do nothing, and then switches that seem to control everything? Ask the sellers how often they trip a breaker. If they are honest, and it's more than once every few months, then the home may not be able to handle a normal power load with today's modern conveniences. Burn marks around electrical outlets is a dead giveaway that this home is a fire hazard.

- Curb appeal—It is important for a home to have great curb appeal. This means that it looks its best and is inviting. Take a look at your potential property from the street. Remember that a clean and simple look can have great impact. Something as easy as planting new grass and trimming the vegetation makes all the difference and is not overly expensive. What can get pricy is replacing a lot of concrete. If the home has a significantly damaged driveway or sidewalks, it can really eat up your budget.

- Roof—It's a well-known truth that every roof is a great roof, until it rains. You must have your roof inspected and be aware that any problems can not only cost you a lot, they can also cause the roof to be excluded from your homeowner's policy. Roof repair is one of those things that is never easy or cheap. I know of very few roofers who will climb on a roof for less than $500, and it escalates quickly from there. Signs of past problems are moisture stains on the ceiling and peeling or warped trim and paint. It is also important to have someone look at the attic and note any varmint activity or problems. Sometimes not much can be seen from the outside, but inside there may be hoards of squirrels running rampant.

So you might wonder, why wouldn't you just buy the best house in the area and forego any problems at all? That's because the best house will also have the biggest price tag, and it won't have the potential to escalate in value as quickly. This is an investment, and the idea is to make money, not just skate by. Most of the ruby-type homes need a little updating, new appliances, and a paint job. These are things that are easily and inexpensively accomplished, and they can add to your long-term investment value.

LET'S MAKE A DEAL

When someone looks at real estate negotiations, it may seem that there is always a winner and a loser. But that is not necessarily the case. You want to buy a house, and they want to sell it. The only thing you need to do to meet each other's needs is to come to agreement on the terms. The whole idea of negotiation in a real estate transaction is to get all of your needs and most of your wants met, and the same is true for the other party. It is really all about finding the win-win situation for everyone.

Since there are so many unknowns that may be factors down the road, many times a buyer will make on offer that depends on certain conditions. This is called a contingency clause. Sometimes these clauses are good, and sometimes they are bad, depending on if you are the buyer or seller. Contingencies are important in real estate contracts because they limit a buyer's or seller's responsibility to fulfill the contract and close the deal should something be discovered about the property that they weren't expecting, or should financing or another sale not happen.

For example, some buyers may want to make an offer to buy a home before they even list their own home for sale. However, in order to come up with the down payment to actually make the purchase, they need to sell their present home. So they make their offer conditional on the successful sale of their own home. If the sellers agree to this contingency, they are basically agreeing to take their home off the market until the other home sells, unless they have an escape clause. I usually advise against accepting a contingency without some kind of escape for the seller. The escape clause allows other buyers the opportunity to entertain offers while keeping the first offer on a time limit.

Another contingency that buyers might want to include is that their purchase is contingent upon their ability to obtain financing. If they can't get the loan, they can't buy the house anyway, so it is a contingency that makes sense. But if you are the seller, you must be aware that this kind of deal will sometimes fall through. Buyers who have not first contacted a lender to find out what kind of loan they can get and what amount might be available to them can waste a great deal of your time.

One of the most common contingencies has to do with inspections, which we talked about in the first part of this chapter. Buyers should want to make sure the property passes these inspections, so they make their offer contingent upon a good report.

Real estate contracts have specific clauses that allow renegotiation in limited areas. For example, a real estate contract may require a buyer to get his home inspection completed in fourteen days. It allows the buyer a specified time, three days for example, to review the inspection and report any problems to the seller. If no problems are reported, that contingency automatically disappears.

But what happens when the inspection is performed within the required time frame, and it shows a small bit of previous termite damage that the buyer reports to the seller? The buyer and seller then renegotiate that aspect of the deal. It's a legal contingency, subject to renegotiation. The seller may decide to fix the damage, or he may decide not to. The buyer then decides whether it is worth losing the house over a little bit of previous damage or not. The seller decides whether it is worth losing a buyer over the issue as well. While this is a minor example, there are times when a major issue is discovered, such as a faulty roof design. That would require more serious thought and substantial renegotiation.

You don't want to be saddled with problems that could have been prevented or pay more than a home might actually be worth given its actual condition. While we know the ideas of contracts and legalese are mind numbing at times, they are very important to be aware of, as you are investing a lot of your hard-earned money. So don't take shortcuts, and make sure you get the best deal possible.

REVIEW

- Maximize gains by finding a home that needs a little work.

- Prioritize a list of characteristics that you want in a home.

- Have realistic expectations for a home in your price range.

- Learn to recognize homes that have potential and those that are a lost cause.

- Steer away from homes that have major issues.

- Negotiation is about finding the win-win situation for both parties.

CASH OR CHARGE?

Your ability to learn faster than your competition is your only sustainable competitive advantage.

—Arie De Gues

You know you want to buy a home. You may even already have one, so you're familiar with how interest works. But you may not really understand how expensive it is over the long term.

Interest is the cost that a bank or mortgage company charges you to borrow their money. Since a home is the biggest purchase that most people ever make, it is extremely rare that you will be able to pay all cash for a home, either as a residence or for investment purposes. For this reason, it is very important to understand the effect that interest has over the long term.

There are numerous types of mortgages that we will discuss a bit later, but for now, let's look at the numbers on some of the most common types to get an idea of how interest can hurt you if you're not careful.

Thirty-year mortgage/6 percent interest/$250,000 house

Principal borrowed: $250,000
Annual payments: twelve
Total payments: 360 (thirty years)
Annual interest rate: 6 percent
Regular payment amount: $1,498.88
Total repaid: $539,596.80
Total interest paid: $289,596.80
Interest as percentage of principal: 115.839 percent

Thirty-year mortgage/7 percent interest/$250,000 house

Principal borrowed: $250,000
Annual payments: twelve
Total payments: 360 (thirty years)
Annual interest rate: 7 percent
Regular payment amount: $1,663.26
Total repaid: $598,773.60
Total interest paid: $348,773.60
Interest as percentage of principal: 139.509 percent

Thirty-year mortgage/8 percent interest/$250,000 house

Principal borrowed: $250,000
Annual payments: twelve
Total payments: 360 (thirty years)
Annual interest rate: 8 percent
Regular payment amount: $1,834.41
Total repaid: $660,387.60
Total interest paid: $410,387.60
Interest as percentage of principal: 164.155 percent

(Calculations from: http://www.bretwhissel.net/cgi-bin/amortize)

There are a couple of very important ideas to note from the preceding examples. Not only does a higher interest rate affect the total amount you will repay over time, it also has a tremendous effect on your payments; in this case a difference of up to $350 per month!

Principal and interest together comprise most of your payment. The total is then divided into equal payments over the life of the loan, using a process called amortization. With amortization, your payments mostly go toward interest early in the loan, and then more goes to principal as the years pass.

For example, if you borrow $100,000 dollars with a thirty-year loan at 7 percent interest, amortization will calculate your payments something like this:

Payment	Amount	Interest	Principal	Balance
First payment	$665	$583	$82	$99,918
At five years	$665	$550	$115	$94,132
At ten years	$665	$501	$164	$85,812
At twenty years	$665	$336	$329	$57,300
Last payment	$665	$4	$661	$0

As you can see, the interest is front loaded, so during those early years, you aren't making much headway on the principal. You also have to remember that your total payment is more than just the principal and interest. The acronym PITI can help you remember all the parts of your payment. It stands for principal, interest, taxes, and insurance.

If you put less than 20 percent down on the loan, the bank or lender considers it a little riskier and requires an escrow account. They pay your annual insurance and taxes from this account and collect money monthly to gather the required amounts.

If you put less than 20 percent down, your lender will probably also require you to include an amount for private mortgage insurance (PMI) in your payment. This is then added to the required principal and interest amounts to total your monthly payment.

FIXED-RATE MORTGAGES

There are various types of mortgages you might have heard about, whether you live in Canada or the United States The most common and prevalent type is fixed-rate mortgages.

Fixed rate means that you pay the same interest rate for the entire life of the loan. Most fixed-rate mortgage loans are for thirty years, although you can also get them for fifteen or twenty years. In Canada, fixed-rate mortgages used to be available for up to forty years, but now, due to the credit crunch, the longest term you can probably get will be thirty-five years.

Shorter loans, such as fifteen- or twenty-year mortgages, usually have lower interest rates, typically one-half or one-quarter of a percent lower than a thirty-year loan, but the total monthly payment will probably still be higher than that of a longer term loan because you have to make bigger payments in order to pay the loan off in the shorter time frame.

You will pay less overall interest with a short-term loan, however, than if you'd borrowed the same amount with a longer loan. Depending on your situation, carefully consider a shorter loan. While a longer loan will generally give you a lower monthly payment, if you can afford the higher payment, you may save a lot of money in the long run and build equity much faster with a shorter loan.

ADJUSTABLE-RATE MORTGAGES

These have become very popular in the United States over the last ten years. This is true, especially in areas where home prices escalated tremendously, like California or Florida. With an adjustable-rate mortgage, your interest rate, and therefore your payment, can go up or down through the life of the mortgage, depending on various economic factors.

The reason that these were so attractive is that the rate begins lower than the rate for a fixed rate mortgage; in the past they've been lower by as much as 2 percent. Though these loans were really popular, they have contributed to much of the housing crises experienced in the United States. As rates were readjusted (most were tied to U.S. treasuries) it caused homeowner monthly payments to rise, and as we've already discussed, that difference could be hundreds of dollars per month!

This is proof that when it sounds too good to be true, it probably is. The adjustable-rate mortgage really only helps you if interest rates stay the same or go down from the time you purchase your home, and they rarely go the direction you'd like.

The main benefit of a fixed-rate mortgage is that your payment remains the same through the life of the loan. This predictability makes planning easier, and they are also much simpler to understand, so you don't have to worry quite so much that something might catch you by surprise.

If you have a fixed-rate loan, in order to take advantage of falling interest rates, you would have to refinance, and that will cost several thousand dollars and require paperwork, and some people are not willing to do that. It's really a no-brainer if you go back and look at the beginning of this chapter at the comparisons of interest rates. In those examples, just a 1-percent drop could lower your monthly payment at least 10 percent and save you more than $50,000 over the life of the loan. Don't you agree that it is worth a little paperwork and a few thousand dollars?

A POINT ABOUT POINTS

When you start talking about points, many home buyers get confused. It is really a pretty simple concept, and understanding it just a little can really help you in the long run.

A point is 1 percent of the loan amount, and lenders can charge from one to several points on a loan to cover their cost of doing business. These are called origination points. Points are paid as part of closing costs.

Discount points are prepaid interest; the more discount points you pay at closing, the lower the interest rate on your mortgage will be. For example, let's say you are buying a $250,000 home with 10 percent down. The closing costs are $5,700, and the loan amount is $225,000. This means a discount point costs $2,250. Do you buy one? Absolutely, and here's why:

That one-point difference in interest will lower your monthly payment by about $170. So you will have earned every dime of that back in a little over one year. Also, it will save you an additional $50,000 over the life of the loan. Now that $2,250 sounds cheap, doesn't it? But coming up with an extra couple of grand at closing can be hard for some people, right?

Here's a big secret: you don't have to use your money! Let's look at an example.

Mike and Mandy are negotiating with Doris and Dan for a beautiful home that Mike and Mandy plan to live in for at least ten years or longer. During negotiations, Dan doesn't want to go any lower than $385,000 on the price of the home. Mike and Mandy can swing that down payment only if the sellers help to cover the closing costs. They check with the mortgage broker and find out that the ballpark estimate of closing costs for their loan is about $6,500. So they call up Dan and Doris's realtor and counter with an offer of the $385,000 if the sellers will pay up to $10,000 in closing costs.

Dan and Doris agree to this arrangement. Since points are considered closing costs, Mike and Mandy ask the broker to add a discount point at closing. This lowers their payment $300 per month and will save them more than $82,000 over the life of the loan, and Dan and Doris paid for it! Discount points are deductible, even if the seller pays them for you.

YOUR CREDIT SCORE

When you apply for a mortgage, the lender will get a copy of your credit report. This report gives all the details about your financial history, payment records, total debt, and any bankruptcies. The information on this report is used by various credit agencies to calculate your credit score (the most common is FICO). This score is an assessment of risk based on several criteria and gives the lender an idea of how likely you are to repay the loan. Credit scores range from 300 to 900, with most people falling somewhere between 600 and 700. Most people need a credit score of at least 640 to be considered by the majority of lenders these days due to the tightening of credit requirement.

The higher your credit score, the more appealing you are to a lender, and the more likely they will be to offer you good rates and loan terms. Factors affecting your credit score include the number and frequencies of your delinquencies, how long you've had credit, and how close you are to your credit limits.

If you know that you will be applying for a mortgage in the near future, it is wise to request a copy of your own credit report in order to clear up any errors or poor history before visiting a lender. It's estimated that almost 80 percent of credit reports contain errors, so it is definitely worth your time to be sure that yours is accurate.

In years past, common wisdom suggested that by closing unused credit accounts, you could improve your credit score. This is absolutely not true! Closing unused accounts lowers your overall available credit and raises your percentage of credit used, which accounts for 30 percent of your credit score. On-time payments can really help you, as that accounts for another 35 percent. Just being aware of these two areas can help you make tremendous strides toward having a really lofty score. The remainder of your score is made up of things that you have less control over:

- Length of credit history 15 percent

- Types of credit used 10 percent

- Recent loans and amounts secured 10 percent

As you can see, the main factors of available credit and payment history account for a whopping 65 percent of your score. That's bad if you habitually pay everything a day late. Remember, one day late is the same as thirty days late. However, if you know how the score works, then you also know that paying everything on time for just a few months in a row can have a very positive impact on your score and take you from renting to owning in a very short period of time.

THE DOWN PAYMENT

Down payments are usually the biggest hurdle for home buyers, especially first-timers. With the days of easy lending drawing to a close, many lenders are being much stricter about requiring larger down payments. Most lenders prefer at least 20 percent down and require at least 5 percent to 10 percent down. Financing a mortgage with less than 20 percent down requires you to get private mortgage insurance. Putting more money down on a house may persuade lenders to overlook credit problems, as well as loan you more money.

There are still some programs around for first-time, or low-income home buyers, but they are becoming fewer all the time. A good realtor can often direct you to programs that can help you get into a home.

But what if you're still turned down? In years past, almost anyone could get any type of loan because the lenders would just adjust the terms for your circumstances. However, with the housing market meltdown in the United States, the days of easy home loans are quickly disappearing. If you are turned down, you still have several options.

1. You can wait until you have a bigger down payment so the lender will overlook some issues.

2. You can ask the lender for a review of the decision. This is especially effective if there were extenuating circumstances that temporarily impacted your finances, such as an illness.

3. You can take some time and repair your credit based on feedback from the lender.

4. You can simply go to another lender, as all lenders operate under slightly different guidelines, and another may look at your situation differently.

5. You can look into seller financing.

REVIEW

- Interest over the long term can really add up.
- Choose a mortgage that's right for you and your situation.
- Fixed-rate mortgages guarantee the same interest rate over the life of the loan.
- Adjustable-rate mortgages reset the interest rate periodically according to current interest rates.
- Discount points are prepaid interest.
- Know your credit score.

EQUITY IS YOUR FRIEND

A billion here and a billion there, and pretty soon you're talking real money.

—Everett Dirksen

The concept of equity can be hard for some people to grasp, but it's really quite simple. Equity is best described as the difference between a home's value and the amount owed on it. This means that equity escalates in two ways: from you making your mortgage payments, thereby decreasing the amount owed, and also from the yearly increase in value of the property.

This means that if your home is currently valued at $350,000 and you owe $250,000, then you have $100,000 in equity. When making this calculation, you must take into account any second mortgages or liens as well, as they count against the value.

Over the past decade especially, many homeowners have seen their equity value escalate, as home prices have soared in some areas. Many tapped into that equity through home equity loans or second mortgages. While this is a great way to access funds, the danger appears if the value of your home declines. You could end up owing more than the home is worth. On the positive side, equity can be put to work to accomplish many of life's goals from making improvements to the home, to paying for college tuition or for business ventures, and even buying additional rental properties.

It is important to remember that your home is the collateral for all the mortgages, lines of credit, or liens that you become involved in, so you must use it wisely. I know of numerous clients who tapped into their home equity to pay off credit cards, and while this action isn't bad in and of itself, a few short months later, they were right back in the same boat, having once again run up those cards. Taking on additional debt to bail yourself out is of no use if you don't have the discipline to break bad financial habits.

I've also seen people take out their home equity to invest in a great money-making idea. This is fine, as long as you can handle the additional payment should that great idea go sour.

When borrowing against your home equity, realize that most lenders cap this type of loan at 75 percent of the home's value. This means that they take 75 percent of the current value, subtract loans and mortgages you already have that use your home as collateral, and the difference is what is available for a home equity loan.

A home equity line of credit can be used at any time for any purpose, but there are several fees associated with a home-equity line of credit. Choose a lender that offers competitive rates and does not eat up a large chunk of your loan with assorted fees. It is a good idea to seek financial advice from a professional before securing a home equity loan or line of credit, since you could lose your home if you fail to repay the amount borrowed.

Borrowing against this equity is currently a very popular method of getting a lump sum of money at low interest rates. When you also take into account that interest on most home equity loans is tax deductible, they become very attractive sources of cash. The vast majority of home equity loans are typically used for consolidating consumer debt or covering a large expense, such as a big wedding, college tuition, or home renovations. Some people also use them to start a business or to invest in rental property.

Given the credit crunch and financial downturn in the economy, in my mind there are only a few very special circumstances that would make you want to look at this type of loan.

1. **Gain some breathing room.**

    Many people accumulated a great deal of different types of debt over the last few years. When finances get tight, you can pull some of the equity out of your home and pay off or pay down this other debt. This will allow you some breathing room to recover. It is very important to understand that once you take this action, you must commit to not repeating the actions that got you into the problem in the first place.

2. **Select renovations.**

    One mistake that people make when they think about renovating is that they put million-dollar features into a $100,000 house. Remember that your home is an investment at its most basic form, and you only want to make renovations that make sense for the area and type of home. For example, if you live in a relatively low income area, putting granite countertops and professional appliances in the kitchen is probably not going to dramatically increase the sale price when you put the home on the market. However, if your house is in a nice part of town and is a little run down, then some top-line features will increase the return on your investment. You should always keep one eye toward resale when contemplating these types of renovations and don't spend the money just because you can.

3. **Investments that produce cash flow.**

    Notice that I didn't just say investments. I don't advocate using home equity money to play the market because there are huge risks to doing that. However, if you are going to make an investment that produces cash flow, like rental property, then it might make sense, depending on your situation. Ideally, you could use your equity in one home to purchase another as a rental. This home could be rented out for enough to cover the mortgage payment, and often will even produce additional cash flow. The great part of this type of income-producing property is that the interest on the mortgage is still tax deductible, the mortgage is now being paid by someone else's money, and the property is gaining in value each year, producing more equity.

Some of the items left off of my list are things that in my opinion have no business being paid for with home equity. A wedding is one example. This is a one-time event, and if you need to use home equity, then you don't have the money for the size of party that you are planning. This goes back to my first point, when I say that you have to get your financial decision making under control. Home equity is long-term debt, and you don't pay for short-term needs with long-term debt. The debt may last longer than the marriage these days!

TYPES OF HOME EQUITY LOANS

There are two basic types of home equity loans that most people are familiar with. A traditional home equity loan is also sometimes referred to as a second mortgage. The lender makes you a loan, and you receive all the money at once, to be paid back in regular monthly payments. Interest accumulates from the day you receive the money.

A new creation in the last decade has been a home equity line of credit. With this type of loan, the lender approves you up to a certain amount but gives you checks to use the money as needed. This means that you only use the money as needed and don't pay any interest until the money is used. This is really helpful if you are renovating, in that you only use small bits of money and pay small interest as you renovate. The amount grows gradually and saves you a lot of interest.

When deciding how much money to allow you to borrow, the lender uses numerous tools and calculations. They base their decision on their estimate of your ability to repay the loan. To make this estimate, they look at your income, your available cash, your debt, and your credit history. There are two debt-to-income ratios that lenders calculate based on the information that you provide on your loan application.

First, they check to see how much of your income would go toward the mortgage payment. This is called the front-end ratio. In Canada, we would call this GDS or gross debt service ratio. This guideline suggests that your total payment—including principal, interest, and escrow payments— should not be more than 28 percent of your gross (pre-tax) monthly salary. Lenders vary on the allowable amount, but most stay around 30 percent. To go above this level is to risk having too much house for your income level. To get a quick idea of what this might be for you, you can take your annual salary and multiply it by .30. Now divide it by twelve. This is the maximum total mortgage payment each month. Let's look at a couple of examples:

Jack makes $70,000, per year, and Jenny makes $42,000 per year. Together they make $112,000. This is their calculation:

$112,000 x .30 = 33,600 / 12 = $2,800 per month.

Marvin is single and makes $65,000 per year. So his calculation would look like this:

$65,000 x .30 = $19,500 / 12 = $1,625 per month.

Your numbers will vary from these, and it's just a rough estimation. The exact numbers will have to come from your lender.

Lenders also check how much of your gross income is required to pay all of your debts combined. This is called your back-end ratio and includes the mortgage as well as car payments, credit card payments, student loans, and child support and alimony payments. In Canada, we call this TDS, or total debt service ratio. Generally speaking, most lenders like this ratio to be about 36 percent, but in some areas with very high real estate values, it might go up over 40 percent.

DON'T GET THE MONEY JUST BECAUSE YOU CAN

Be careful when you are discussing percentages and norms with a lender. Just because they say you should be able to afford a house or anything else, it doesn't mean you have to borrow the maximum amount you qualify for. Get what you need, but don't just buy something big because you can. Real estate agents and lenders make more commission on bigger houses and will naturally encourage you to borrow as much as you can.

Stop and think about your lifestyle and what you really want. Would you rather have huge house payments or the ability to travel or save for those special events? You don't want to come to resent your home because you are no longer to go out to eat once in a while. And don't forget that there are always those things that come up, and not having good cash flow can force you to put unexpected expenses on credit cards. This is never the optimal solution.

When thinking about how much home you can afford, some use an old rule of thumb that you should not buy a house that costs more than two and a half times your current salary. One of the factors that could be an issue in how much house you can afford is the fact that lenders in Canada have been less inclined to make loans to just anyone. You may need a bigger down payment and a higher credit score to enter the housing market at all.

OWNER FINANCING

So what is a wannabe homeowner or investor to do if he doesn't fit within the new restrictions? There are still options, though they come with a bit more risk. Owner financing is when the person who owns the home personally carries your mortgage rather than a traditional lender. This means that you may circumvent numerous restrictions on down payment and credit scores, but it also means that you will probably pay more in interest and not have the same protections as you would with a traditional loan.

Asking a seller to give you owner financing to buy a home can be a tricky proposition. That's partly because if you ask the listing agent if the owner will carry some or all of the financing, the agent probably doesn't know. Why? The agent never asked. Remember that realtors are commissioned sales people, so owner financing may mean less commission for them.

If you ask the seller directly, the seller is likely to say no. Sellers often reject the suggestion of owner financing because nobody has explained the benefits or proposed owner financing as a way to sell the home. Most sellers don't sell homes frequently, so they only know about the traditional practices in real estate transactions. But there are times when homes aren't selling in some areas or new credit restrictions are put in place (like now), that seller financing becomes very popular. When the market turns to a buyer's market with a glut of available housing, owner financing can mean the difference between selling a home or sitting on it for months or years.

There are some investors who specialize in seller financing. I know of a man named John, who has accumulated more than 50 homes, most at auction for a fraction of their value, and he has owner financed them all for buyers who have been shut out of the traditional market. He earns a much higher percentage on his investment than he could ever get in the stock market. He occasionally has a borrower default and has to foreclose, but then he is able to resell the house at its new value to a new owner, and so he is compensated for any loss or legal fees. He has made a fortune by specializing in this market.

On the flip side of John's experience, I also know a young couple who had a very bad experience with owner financing. They purchased a home from a man who seemed trustworthy. Two years later, they discovered he had skipped town with their money, and the lender that he had owed his original mortgage to had foreclosed on the home. This couple was out on the street with nothing to show for all the money they had paid and no home. While this can be the answer for some, it is not to be considered lightly.

HOW IT WORKS

You can owner finance all or some of the purchase price of a home. The buyer and seller both sign an agreement that outlines their obligations and recourse. It doesn't matter if the property has an existing loan, except to the extent that the existing lender might accelerate the loan upon sale due to something known as an alienation clause. Not all loans have this clause, but some do. The buyer and seller must agree on terms such as the interest rate, monthly payment, and term of the loan. It is important that this security instrument or agreement be recorded in the public records to protect both parties.

Buyers and sellers are generally free to negotiate the terms of the owner financing, subject to usury laws and other state-specific regulations to prevent the seller from grossly overcharging or taking advantage of the buyer. With owner financing, there is no standard payment required, but most sellers will want an amount from as little as 5 percent to 30 percent or more to protect themselves and their equity. Buyers are much more reluctant to default if they have a significant amount of money at stake.

There are several variations on owner financing, and one of the more common is the lease-purchase. This is often called "rent to own" by some in the real estate business. The buyer signs a lease that contains an agreement to obtain a traditional mortgage at the end of the lease. The buyers are given credit for some of their lease payments toward the price of the home.

While owner financing should be approached with caution, it can offer numerous benefits to home buyers who might otherwise not be able to purchase a home.

These benefits are summarized here:

- **More manageable down payments**

    With lender requirements for down payments rising, in an owner-financing situation, the down payment is negotiable. Even if the seller wants a down payment larger than the buyer would prefer, he might agree to allow the buyer to make large periodic payments along with the house payment to get the down payment paid. One of the biggest obstacles for new buyers is the size of the down payment, and with owner financing, this can be worked out with both parties to everyone's satisfaction.

- **Fewer credit requirements**

    Even if the seller insists on getting the buyer's credit report, the seller's interpretation of buyer qualifications is typically less stringent and more flexible than those imposed by most lenders. The buyer will also have the chance to explain any extenuating circumstances, such as an extended illness, that may have affected his credit negatively.

- **A buffet of financing options**

    Unlike traditional lenders, sellers and buyers who go the owner-financing route can choose from a variety of payment options, such as interest only, graduated payment, and periodic lump sums. Payments can be mixed and matched. Interest rates can adjust periodically based on payment history or remain at one rate for the term of the loan. There are few options that would not work; it's just up to both parties to find what works for that particular situation.

- **Reduced closing costs**

    Traditional lenders must make money when they give you a loan, which is why they charge points. With owner financing, these don't have to exist, and neither do origination fees, processing fees, and any of the other fees that lenders generally tack on at closing to increase their bottom line. This helps everyone by lowering the cost for the buyer to get into the house.

- **Have keys, will travel**

    Don't you hate that long wait while your loan paperwork is processed before you can close on the house and move in? Because buyers and sellers aren't waiting on a lender to process the financing, buyers can close faster and move in to enjoy their new home within days, not weeks or months.

In case you might think that owner financing mostly benefits the buyer, there are also numerous benefits to a seller who considers selling his home with owner financing.

- **More money, honey!**

    One of the perks of offering seller financing is the ability to ask, and get, full price for the home. In some cases, sellers can even ask a premium price since they are able to finance the property, and more buyers will be interested. The value of a buyer being able to negotiate much better terms (such as a lower down payment or fewer credit restrictions) is worth a tremendous amount to those who may not be able to get a home at all under normal circumstances.

- **Additional monthly income and tax benefits**

    Payments from the buyer increase the seller's cash flow on a monthly basis and also allow the seller to only report income from the installments each year rather than on the full amount of the house.

- **Greater return on investment**

    Owner financing can carry a higher rate of interest than a seller might receive in other investments. Typically in a home loan, the interest is front-loaded, meaning a higher amount of each payment is interest. This reverses in the latter years of the loan. The buyer's equity grows slowly, as he pays over time, protecting the seller's equity should the buyer default.

- **Quicker turnaround**

    Owner financing attracts a different crowd of buyers and more of them. If a property is not selling under conventional methods, offering owner financing is one way to make your property stand out from all the others and move a hard-to-sell property that otherwise might not sell.

Though seller financing offers numerous options that can be beneficial to both buyer and seller, it is very important to take the time to check out the details and talk to a good real estate attorney before getting into this arrangement.

I'm sure that you'll notice by the content of this chapter that with real estate, the only real limits are those that you set in your own mind. You can build an empire by buying and selling properties, investing in rentals, or owner financing a whole slew of properties. Though many people will frown on anything that is less than straight-up conventional, they are also not the ones making millions in real estate. Before you take their advice, look at their results, and only listen to those who have been there and done it.

REVIEW

- Get your financial decision making under control.

- Don't tap equity to pay debt.

- Equity in a home can create wealth quickly.

- Don't borrow more than 30 percent of your income in the form of mortgages or home equity loans.

- Owner financing can be your path to home ownership.

- The only real limits are those you set in your mind.

Chapter 7

MOVIN' ON UP

Success is not the key to happiness. Happiness is the key to success. If you love what you are doing, you will be successful.

—Albert Schweitzer

I've spoken to many people who have made a great deal of money in real estate, and there is a lot to learn from these individuals. You can learn not only about making money, but also about the attitude and outlook it takes to go after your goals and achieve them. Your goal may be to buy your dream home, not to be a real estate investor. This is a great goal, and many of the principles of goal setting and creative thinking that I will talk about will definitely help you to achieve it.

Getting what you want in business or in life depends on your perspective. If you think that money or the pursuit of a fabulous lifestyle is bad, then you will never improve your situation. Money is just a thing, a commodity. It only makes you more of what you already are. It doesn't change you. If you are a good person, it will make you a great person, and if you are a bad person, more money will probably just make you a rotten person.

My cousin, Bob Proctor, says, "The best thing you could do for poor people is to not become one of them." In other words, if you want to help others, help yourself first. You cannot give what you do not have, and being able to help your family and friends live better and worry less about money is a fabulous achievement. So, what is holding you back? Why have you not been able to accomplish as much as you may have wanted to thus far?

It is natural for all of us to compare ourselves to people we know and interact with. Most of us carry around the idea that we are average, meaning that we are within a range of lifestyle that is comfortable and comparable to our friends, neighbors, parents, and siblings. What it really means is that we are limiting ourselves through comparison to others. As long as we fall within this perceived range, we don't strive very hard to get to the next level.

We create within our own minds an idea of what is obtainable rather than what is possible. This can be a big problem when we try to set goals because we start out by deciding what is obtainable, and this places you inside a box. We then take steps to achieve the limited goal that is inside that box. A good example would be if you own a modest home and believe that your next home will be a step up, but not a huge step. Conventional wisdom is that you trade up in housing throughout your life, eventually getting to the level of a very nice home. But who says you have to do it that way? Why can't you take a big step up and live in your dream house now? I'm not saying it's easy, but then easy just gets you average anyway, so why choose easy? I'm encouraging you to think creatively and position yourself to take advantage of opportunities when they present themselves.

One of the biggest obstacles most people use as an excuse is time. There never seems to be enough of it. But we all have the same amount of time every single day. This means that you and the billionaire down the street both have the same amount of time, but he knows how to make the most of his, and you don't. He can set his goals and achieve them, whereas most people want to set goals, so they think about doing it, but they don't follow through. Consequently, they never achieve near as much as they could.

THE MIND-SET OF INVESTORS

I talk to numerous people who want to get into the real estate investment business. One of the most difficult things for those making the transition from working for someone else to becoming a real estate investor is the issue of time management. Juggling all of the responsibilities, especially early in the process, can be daunting. If you learn nothing else from this chapter, then learn this: Treat your investing as a business.

To really have the mind-set of someone who is successful, you must devote a specified time schedule to your real estate investing and portfolio. Constantly read and be aware of what is happening in the market and in your local area. While you shouldn't try to time the market, realize that life situations, circumstances, and normal occurrences such as divorce, relocation, upsizing, and downsizing, never change in any market, and they always present opportunities for the savvy investor. The whole idea is not to just stumble your way through investing in real estate, but to become knowledgeable, be in the right place all the time (not just sometimes), and be able to pull the trigger on a great deal. If you have a specified time each day to focus on your business, there is less chance that you will miss the opportunities.

If you believe that you will be successful, you will be. What thought first came to mind when you read that statement? Agreement? Skepticism? Disbelief? Part of the mind-set of an investor involves believing that you can do it and keeping a positive attitude about your results.

Over the past few years, the Law of Attraction has received a lot of media attention. You hear about it on talk shows and in books. The whole premise is that you can attract the things that you want into your life instead of going out and chasing them. However, it is important to understand that the Law of Attraction is and has always has been at work in your life, though you may have been completely unaware of it. It works in both positive and negative ways, depending on your own mind-set.

The basic explanation of this law is the idea that everything that comes into our lives has been attracted by our thoughts. The Law of Attraction is always at work, and everything that happens to us—good, bad, or indifferent—we have attracted, even though we might never understand why.

What this means is that you have the power to bring into your life those great and wonderful things that you have dreamed about—a successful business, great relationships, and peace of mind. Now think about your current mind-set. Are you a disbeliever who is skeptical of these kinds of ideas? Maybe you even tried it before, but it didn't work, so you're now convinced that a positive mind-set does nothing but bring about disappointment. If this is true of your experience, then you must know that the Law of Attraction works at all times in your life, whether you believe in it or not. A skeptical, pessimistic attitude brings about more of the same, while a positive, go-getter attitude improves your results exponentially.

It is important to remember that the Law of Attraction does not discriminate or judge; it can create good results or it can create bad results in equal measure. It doesn't have an opinion; it simply gives you what you focus on, not want you say you want, but what you focus on. So if you sit around on your couch eating bags of potato chips, griping about your lot in life, you will continue to experience crappy results. But if you get your butt off that couch and look for positive and creative ways to get what you want, your life will change. It's really a very simple idea that most of us learned in grammar school, but somehow we gave up on it as adults. You have the power to change your circumstances. You simply have to want to do it.

If you want to use the Law of Attraction in your favor, then you must first take a good, hard look at your present results. This doesn't mean that you should feel bad about them, because we know that feeling bad about something will just attract more of the same. You should do the best you can to stand back and take an objective view.

Ask yourself, "What kind of friends do I currently have? What kind of coworkers? How do I feel about my level of income? How is my business going?" As the answers to these questions flash through your mind, write them down. It is important to write the first answer that pops into your head, not the white lie you tell everyone else. Write those thoughts down, and then take a look at them.

It is very common for people who try this exercise to dislike the thoughts and ideas that are revealed. Most people have a list of negatives that spill forward as well as excuses. "I can't make big money. I have no idea how to even start." "That's not for me. I've worked hard to get where I am, and I can't add more stuff." "No one like me does this kind of thing." "Why would I want to rock the boat, we're barely surviving now." "Everyone I know would think I was nuts if I tried it."

Know right up front that these thoughts are just a reflection of what has happened in your life. You have the ability to change things if you choose to. After you take stock of where you are and take responsibility for what has produced your results, you are ready to move forward.

So what if you tried the positive mind-set idea before but didn't see any results? Many people have this experience, and the main reason they don't see immediate and lasting results is that they still must live and work in the same environment as before. Odds are, the majority of people you are around in a given day aren't all positive and supportive. It doesn't take long for them to affect your positive attitude and drag it back down, and that's when you don't get the results you want.

For example, if you have a friend or family member who is constantly spouting a stream of negative thoughts—complaining about her job, her relationships, her lack of money—then it may completely destroy your attempts at a positive outlook. How many times have you noticed that after being with this person that you felt physically drained? It's like she hooked up a vacuum to your brain and sucked the life right out of you.

The only sure way to correct this problem is to stay away from that person, but since we don't always choose our family members and business contacts, it isn't always practical. If you are in this situation, then the best way to protect yourself is to shift the conversation to something positive. If you refuse to commiserate with this type of person, it lessens the impact of her negative thoughts and allows your more positive ones to shine through.

Until you recognize where the thoughts came from that created your results, and choose to change those thoughts, you won't make much progress toward your goals of improving your financial status through real estate investing or buying that dream home. Once you understand them, it then takes a strong desire to change, and the best way to do that is to set effective goals.

GOAL SETTING 101

You have probably been setting goals in some way since you were a young child. We are taught early on that we can measure our productivity and accomplishments, but to reach the really big goals, we must set little goals like stepping stones. School days are full of setting goals and working hard getting to the next level. But then we find ourselves on our own, and somehow those principles that we've been working with for so long aren't translated into our daily lives. In fact, it's almost like we forgot how to set goals at all.

This is gut-wrenchingly common, and it's why so many people get to their twilight years wondering where all the time went and why they have to struggle. By allowing our dreams to be tempered by those around us, we are putting ourselves in that average box again. Unfortunately, if you have a goal that is average, that often means that your results will be below average, so you don't even keep pace, let alone improve your life.

Rather than pursue a goal or dream, many people take what is at hand and what is easy, and try to carve out a happy life from what life hands them. They don't strive toward something; they only muddle through with what they are given. This can happen with your job, your relationships, and even your health, and it happens before you even realize it, if you aren't paying attention.

Goal setting can be a tricky business. While you don't want to be completely off the charts into fantasyland, you also don't want to set your sights too low. No one is going to give you everything you want, just because you decided you want it. You will have to work for it, sacrifice, and be willing to put in 100 percent, no matter what obstacles stand in your way.

Writing down your goals is an important part of the process. Though many people set goals once a year, at New Year's or on their birthdays, they usually shove them in a drawer and don't even look at them until the next year. But even those people are way ahead of those who set no goals at all.

A good life takes active planning and participation, and even if you're the once-a-year kind of goal setter, then that's better than nothing. In order to move forward as quickly as possible, it pays to revisit your goals on a weekly and monthly basis. Then at the end of the year you can be pleasantly shocked at how far you've come in such a short time, rather than feeling depressed at having the same goals for the next year because you didn't get anywhere.

So what makes a good goal? Even if you have an idea at this point of what you want out of your real estate investment, or what you want in that dream home, how do you write that down in a way that will be achievable? An effective goal has certain identifiable elements:

1. It is clear and specifically defined.

2. It is achievable in the given time frame.

3. It is disciplined.

4. It is aligned with other short-term or long-term goals.

5. It is flexible in terms of acceleration or escalation.

Let's take the first one: clear and specifically defined goals. You might say to yourself, "I want to retire at age fifty," or "I want to have all the money I need." While those are great ideas, they aren't specific, so you can't measure them to see exactly where you are at. A better way to phrase this goal might be, "I want to make $5 million in real estate, so I can retire at age fifty and not worry about having enough money."

Most people respond better to very specific goals than they do to plans to "do better" or "be the best." A good goal will tell you how, when, where, and by what means you are going to reach your goals, so you can track your progress.

For example, if you are going to make $5 million and retire by the age of fifty, then you need to investigate and list some possibilities that will make it happen. They might include: buying X (number) of properties each year to own as rentals or to flip, or owner financing X (number) of houses. It might include choosing properties that have the potential for double-digit appreciation or higher than average rents. You must be creative and read and learn as much as possible. A good way to do this is to listen to and learn from those who have done it before you. The big real estate barons of our day, as well as any local investors you know who have done well, are people who will help you find innovative ideas to add to your goals to get you to your $5 million faster than you can imagine.

When I sit down with someone to work on their goals, I find that many people will confuse goals and tasks. Goals are the big achievements, and tasks are the small, baby steps that you work on every day to get closer to that big achievement. For example, if your goal is to buy one rental property every month, then a task might be meeting with your realtor each week to go over potential properties. Accomplishing small tasks toward your goal every day is important because it gives you a sense of control and achievement. However, be sure that all the small tasks keep you working toward the goal. It is very easy to seem busy, but in reality you might be sitting still. Write down each activity on the path to your goal, and evaluate it on a weekly or monthly basis. This will tell you if you are spending too much time on things that aren't moving you forward and producing the desired results.

LONG-TERM AND SHORT-TERM GOALS

Everyone needs both short- and long-term goals. Some short-term goals are based on a sense of urgency, for example, cleaning up your credit in the next six months. Others are larger stepping stones to reach your long-term goals.

So why not just make the big, long-term goals, and do away with all of these short-term goals? Humans are needy creatures, and the truth is that we perform better with regular and consistent reinforcement. So use these short-term goals to give yourself a pat on the back and keep going. As you track your progress and see how many short-term goals you have accomplished, it makes the long-term goals seem that much closer and easier to reach.

Long-term goals have a very important function, as well. In addition to giving you an overall direction, they also provide a focal point when times get hard or you suffer setbacks. Focusing on the long-term goal and being able to see the big picture can get you through those times when it would be easy to quit. It allows you to see your situation as temporary and gives you the will to search for solutions. As you overcome each difficulty, it builds the confidence that you will need to push on toward that long-term goal.

So how do you start setting your goals? I have designed a worksheet that will help you focus on your goals and teach you how to break them down into bite-sized chunks. Then we will further break them down into individual tasks. You will want to alter this form to suit your own needs and goals, but you must write them down and track them. I'm going to use a few examples for this worksheet so you can see how it flows.

GOAL WORKSHEET

Long-term goal:

1. Make $5 million in the next twenty years with real estate investments.

   A. **Short-term goals (STGs) related to long-term goal**

   1. Frequently check and clean up credit to get best interest rates.

   2. Pay off credit cards and put money in savings for down payments.

   3. Start accumulating properties using alternative financing, such as owner financing.

   B. **Tasks to achieve short-term goals to work on this week**

   1. Pull consolidated credit report from all three credit agencies and find out credit score.

   2. Decided which credit cards have the highest interest rates and pay those down first.

   3. Check the local Sunday paper to find owners willing to carry the financing on their properties.

This example gives you an idea of how the long-term goals and short-term goals are interrelated and how the daily tasks move you along on each of the goals. You can make this as simple or as complicated as you like; just don't get stuck in the planning stage!

Procrastination is a big pile of dynamite when it comes to reaching your goals. This is why so many people get to the end of the year and realize that the goals they set last year didn't budge an inch. They put off working on them each week, then each month, until a whole year has passed. The world keeps moving forward, whether you do or not, and by standing still, you get left further and further behind.

I know very few people who aren't motivated when they set their goals. The problem is that you have to sustain that motivation. This happens when you have to choose goals that are within your realm of control and within a doable timetable. What does this mean?

Let's say that you decide that you currently schlep burgers for a living. It's not a bad living, just an average one. But then you decide that you want to fly tour helicopters in Las Vegas and own a casino by this time next year. While you may be able to accomplish both of these goals in the long term, the timetable of a year is probably unrealistic. You have to have certain skills and certifications for these particular goals that take time to earn. This is what I mean by choosing goals within your realm of control and achievable for your chosen time frame.

Just as it is unrealistic to think that you can lose fifty pounds in a month and keep it off, it is also unrealistic to think that you can make $1 million dollars in a year in real estate and have any idea how to keep the money. Can you make $1 million? Sure, many people do, once they know the game and are able to get big-time leverage.

This may happen quickly for you, or a little more slowly, but it won't be overnight. You have to put in the time and effort to learn the business, and it will pay off for you in the end. I'm not saying you can't get lucky and hit a jackpot property, but just don't bet the farm on it.

While it may seem that all this planning and thinking about your goals is wasting time that you could spend achieving them, it is not. Remember, I said that knowing what not to do is almost as important as knowing what to do. Learning from others and from mentors saves time by allowing you to avoid the setbacks and learn from their experiences. Every pitfall you can avoid is time saved toward achieving your long-term goal.

Rex and Connie have invested in real estate for the past fifteen years and have made many mistakes. Rex tells the story:

> "We started investing in rental property when we were first starting out, and then we had the twins. Connie had a finance degree, and real estate management is really flexible, so it allowed her to be more available to the girls. We started with a couple of properties and had some really bad experiences right off the bat. We bought houses that were in really bad shape and rented them to the wrong people. Every problem seemed like it cost more than we ever got in rent, and it felt like an absolute pit. We both ended up working full time just to cover the cash outlay on the properties. We felt our girls were almost parentless those first few years as we spent all of our extra time at the properties.
>
> It got so bad that we felt like we were just digging a pit of debt and not making anything. I was complaining to my dad one day about the mess we were in, and he suggested that I go talk to a real estate broker who had been investing in his own properties for years. I did. He showed us what we had done wrong and the steps we needed to take to fix our errors and make our real estate profitable. It took us five years to get things on track and really start making money. Now the girls are in college, and we have great income from our properties. But it took us five years of financial nightmare.
>
> If we had taken the time to sit down with someone who had experience before we jumped into real estate, we could have saved ourselves years of worry and struggle, not to mention thousands of dollars. If I have any advice for anyone, it is to do your homework and save the heartache."

Many obstacles can and will get in your way as you strive for your goals. But by studying where you want to go and how you are going to get there, it gives you a solid path to follow and helps you avoid problems that can cost you a bundle.

The flip side of setting unrealistic goals is to set goals that are too low. Something that is easily attainable hardly qualifies as a goal at all. Try not to underestimate yourself or discount the skills that you have. As a general rule, people become easily bored with a goal that is too easily met. They lose interest, and you will, too.

You must pick goals that challenge you professionally, mentally, and even spiritually. Go for the deals that make you stretch your possibilities and require a high level of creativity and energy to meet.

You will never achieve great things without pushing yourself. Goals that don't push you forward move you sideways. They do not get you out of your comfort zone or force you to learn new and difficult things. It takes two key factors to reach any goal: commitment and adaptability.

Commitment to your goal means that you take the necessary steps, whatever those may be, to achieve it. You are creating self-imposed deadlines for specific tasks and evaluating your own progress. You crack your own whip. You develop the next set of strategic tasks to move forward. The first step of committing to the process is to write down your goal. The second step is to announce it to people you know. This may seem like you are giving those around you the opportunity to rip you to shreds. Some people may do that, but by first writing your goal down and then announcing it to others, you have additional motivation because you know people will be asking about your progress at every function, event, and family gathering. This forces you to not only be accountable to yourself but also to others.

You have probably heard people close to you announce their plans, but how did they do it? Did they say, "I'm going to lose thirty pounds and compete in a triathlon by this time next year," or did they say something like, "After the holidays, I'm going to lose weight, and then I'll be able to do what I want?"

If you heard someone make the first statement, you would assume that they are serious and committed to their goals. However, if you heard the second statement, you might wonder how serious they were or if this was just a pipedream. This person, instead of setting a goal and being willing to work hard to get what he wants, is content to just wish and get nowhere. Here again, procrastination is your enemy. If you are thinking that you will start working toward you real estate investment goals after the holidays, on your birthday, or after such and such happens, you are just blowing smoke. Every day that you waste is a day wasted. You don't get it back, and you don't get do-overs. Get to work, or get out of the way.

The second key factor to reaching your goal is adaptability. This is about how you deal with circumstances. You must use your creativity to overcome obstacles and listen to feedback. This will help you fine-tune your goals. You must have the ability to step back on a regular basis (I recommend at least monthly) and evaluate your progress. What worked? What didn't? What changes are you going to make in your task list for next month?

Goal planning involves some risk on your part. That means risking a wrong move, a bad decision, and even a major setback. It also means that you must be flexible to changing circumstances. You must still juggle job, family, and bills in addition to striving toward your investment goals. There are times when certain goals will take a backseat to others temporarily, out of necessity, but all of these instances give you the opportunity to be creative and perhaps even come up with another opportunity that fits into your long-term plan.

Feedback is important because no matter how well you have researched or planned, there may be some areas that you have overlooked or are unaware of. You may also lose your perspective from time to time and be unable to figure out what you're doing wrong. At those times, a wise or experienced friend or mentor can help you get back on track.

THE PANIC ATTACK

I'd be lying to say that there won't be times when it's a little scary, and you feel out of your element and in way over your head. Everyone has the odd panic attack now and then, when you doubt your abilities and are tempted to run back to that comfort zone that you are so familiar with. This can be enhanced if you are grilled by Aunt Bessie about how things are going in the middle of Thanksgiving dinner. Family and friends may tell you everything that you can't do and discourage you from moving forward or even trying. You have to remember to focus on your plan. This means not letting your emotions get the best of you to the point that you try to prove everyone wrong. While harsh comments and criticism might motivate you to strive toward your goals, they may also lead you into the pit of self-sabotage when you allow others to affect your plan. You might try to accelerate your plan to prove something and can easily end up with less than you started with.

You must guard yourself against this kind of reaction. Stick to your plan and avoid the traps. If you blow it, start again. Build on what you have and learn from each lesson. One of Newton's laws of physics is that an object in motion stays in motion, while an object at rest stays at rest. The same is true for the human mind. If you feel in control and like you are making progress, then it is easier to keep going. However, if you feel out of control and allow that feeling to let you come to a stop, then it takes even more effort to get going again. You are most certainly your worst critic. Leave your mistakes in the past and continue to move forward.

REVIEW

- Money is just a thing. It is a commodity that does not define you.

- Think creatively and go for what is possible instead of what is probable.

- Treat your investing as a business.

- You have the ability to change.

- Write down your goals and revisit them often.

- Both long- and short-term goals are essential for success.

IT AIN'T HARD, JUST DIFFERENT

I know the price of success: dedication, hard work, and an unremitting devotion to the things you want to see happen.

—Frank Lloyd Wright

There are those who seek to become wealthy through property investment. However, with the recent mortgage crisis and resulting credit crunch, they may find that their fears prevent them from giving it serious consideration. While the landscape of property investing has shifted a bit, it is still a very good way to accumulate wealth. One of the biggest secrets of real estate wealth is that the best time to buy is when everyone else is selling, and in many markets, it is a buyer's market. This means that there are many more homes for sale than there are buyers, so sellers are willing to make deals and offer very attractive terms. But before you jump into the property market, you have to know yourself very well.

THE INVESTOR MIND-SET

The mind-set of the investor is probably the most important aspect of property investing. You can have all the information necessary on investment techniques, but unless you are ready for it, you most likely won't do anything about it. Mind-set is all about knowing that you deserve to be successful and happy. Property investing isn't something that is done by rich, greedy, heartless people wanting to be slumlords; that's only an excuse put out there by people not wanting to be successful and ensuring that they have a valid reason for it.

I have found that the mind-set of success is about making good choices, having a solid direction with specific goals, and having the persistence of will to make it happen. Everything you do or don't do is a choice. Your own financial results are completely within your control. No matter what you say to try to convince yourself or those around you that your situation is not your fault, everything you have ever done was done because you chose to do it. Now that can be an empowering and even scary thought about events that have happened in your life, but your reaction to those events and what you believe those events mean is completely your choice. Even if right now you are skeptical that you could really become a property investor, you have the choice to learn the secrets and join the elite crowd of successful people or not.

A good, solid direction is also something you must have to obtain what you want. You must set long-term and short-term goals and make them a priority. Though you will occasionally need to tweak your direction, trying something for a few months, then going in a completely different direction is very counterproductive. You only gain momentum by building on the goals that you have already met, and this is completely lost if you ditch that path and try something else. If you don't know where you are going, how are you going to know how to get there, let alone when you get there? You must know what your goal is and what steps you need to take to get there. You must also know where you are now. Be honest with yourself about this, and if you need to work on you first, then do it, and get moving to what you want.

Persistence sounds like it's a lot of work and that it might be hard. It can be, but it can also be a fun journey. There will be challenges, and often things don't happen instantly, they take some time. How you face the challenges is determined by your attitude and will to succeed. As long as you keep your mind focused on the outcome you want, you will find the creative solutions that you need to fix any problem. Stay focused on what you want, visualize what it will feel like when you get there, and keep moving toward it.

Much of the experiences you have, both positive and negative, are entirely dependent on your perspective, and property investing is no different. If you are thinking at this very moment in time that things are too hard, or that this kind of thing never works out for you, then imagine yourself in ten or even thirty years' time. Are you going to think back and say, "I am glad I chose to get started in property investment," or are you going to be there saying, "If only I'd taken that step to get started in investing instead of depending on my job, then I'd have choices instead of feeling vulnerable."

It seems to make a huge difference when you see it years into the future, and that's because you are allowing yourself to have a different perspective. Stop looking at your situation right now or what might have happened in the past, and shift your focus to what you can achieve in the future.

The best thing about property investing is that it can provide long-term security. It provides cash flow as well as capital appreciation. It seems that no matter what you read or hear on TV these days, everyone has a strategy or proven system for making money. There are literally endless ways to become a millionaire through investments of all kinds, but that does not mean that every investment is for you. Even though all investors are trying to make money, each one comes from a different background, education level, and experience, and each investor also has different needs and objectives. Property investing is relatively simple and is a tangible investment. Everyone needs a place to live, and you can provide that. There are not any certifications or advanced education needed. But there are things you must be willing to learn, and not everyone likes what is required to be a good property investor.

YOUR INVESTMENT PERSONALITY

There are certain types of investments that suit you, and the way that you find them is to understand two incredibly basic things about yourself: your own investment objectives and your investing personality.

A person's investment personality reflects the amount of risk that he or she is comfortable with. You may want to invest in a stock that everyone thinks is the best thing since sliced bread. But if you worry about it and cannot sleep at night, then it is not the right investment for you. Conversely, if you find yourself looking at the returns on your retirement accounts and feeling frustrated, then you are most likely invested too conservatively.

Just like there are those who like to skydive and those who will not even step on an airplane, the types of investors run the gamut from overly conservative to extremely risky. While you may be a little uncomfortable at first with some kinds of investments, as you gain more experience, you will notice that your risk tolerance can change as well.

Real estate investing can be different things to different people. If someone has had a bad experience or lost money, he may try his best to discourage you from doing the same. Those who have made millions in real estate will tell you that you can't fail. But it really depends on you. Real estate investing takes time, and it doesn't make you money if you sit on the couch and do nothing. It takes effort and the willingness to understand the market.

The most frightening circumstance for many investors is to see a huge drop in the market as some areas have seen with real estate lately. You must know how much volatility you can stand before you start losing sleep; unfortunately, the only way most people find out is through trial and error. Because we have so many emotional attachments to money, the whole subject of risk can be confusing. You may consider yourself an adventurous person in every way, but when it comes to money, you have an unreasonable fear of loss. This could be due to any number of experiences or ideas that you may have been taught as a child. For example, it could be due to financial losses you have suffered in the past.

A good example of this mind-set can be illustrated by many of the people in my grandmother's generation. Having gone through the 1920s and 1930s, they had many very conservative ideas about money and a big distrust of credit. The experiences they had and circumstances that they lived through shaped this mind-set, just as the circumstances and events in your life have shaped yours.

RISK AND REWARD

Risk is all about expectations. Take the example of commuting to and from work. It bears a certain risk. You leave your house expecting to arrive at work on time. Anything can happen, from an accident to road construction to traffic jams, but if you travel the road frequently enough, you come to know the risks and still arrive almost every day at the same time. The point is that we become familiar and comfortable with these elements of risk because we have learned gradually over years of commuting to accept them and understand when things happen that might interfere with our objective. We do not stop and turn around at the first sign of a problem.

It is a well-known fact that you have a much higher chance of being killed in a car accident than in an airplane crash. Yet, how many times does the risk of death cross your mind when you go out and hop in your car? On the other hand, how many times have you encountered a little turbulence on a flight and silently hoped the airplane would not crash? Your perception of risk outweighs the reality of the risk, and many people find that their ideas of financial risk are similarly out of line with the true risk that it represents. This is due in part to the fact that we are so used to the risks associated with driving. We have done it so much that we feel in control and are more than willing to accept the risk.

Not only is investing about risk, it is about reward. The key to obtaining your optimal risk opposed to reward balance is a gradual investment approach. Do not start by jumping off a cliff. Start small, with one property, and then reevaluate how it's going every three to six months, while keeping your eyes open for another good property. I frequently recommend that a beginning or inexperienced property investor try this progressive investing strategy, and then take the investing process at your own pace. Gather experience before moving on to riskier properties and understand what you feel comfortable with.

Just like most aspects of life, it is good to get your feet wet before you dive right in. Before you buy a large apartment complex, it is best to try an investment property that will be easier to manage, such as a single-family rental home.

The advantages of learning the tricks of the trade with a relatively inexpensive investment property are not always so obvious. To begin with, an investment property, such as a small rental home, offers a small financial footprint. The price of learning the business and potentially failing is, therefore, much smaller than it would be if you started out with a million-dollar apartment complex. Even if the venture to manage a rental home doesn't work out for you and you decide to exit this particular real estate investment strategy, more than likely you will recoup most of your money on the sale of the property. You stand to lose some money, make no mistake, but it won't be enough to break the bank.

On the other hand, if you decided to dive right into the investment property business, then you must have the financial resources to make a few mistakes. Should things go awry and you are forced to sell the million-dollar property, even a small 5 to 10 percent loss on the investment could result in long- term financial damages to you and your plan. There is much to learn with property investments, and experience is the best teacher, so start small and learn those lessons while they have little impact on your overall finances.

I know many people whose first investment home is their own home. When they move up to a larger and better home, they keep their other property and use it as a rental. Since they already know the property intimately, there are no surprises as they might have with an unknown property. They also know the neighborhood and the neighbors, so they will quickly hear of any problems or strange activity.

Starting off with this kind of small investment property can also help you to become a better property manager. It is easier to adequately address the needs of just one tenant than it is to try to solve the problems of several tenants at once. Part of making an investment property successful is adding value to the rental. If you can learn how to please one tenant, then you will be in a better position to extend what you have learned and please all the tenants in a larger complex. This experience is knowledge that you just can't buy.

When you invest in a single-family dwelling, your financial investment is relatively low. This financial investment allows you to try a few things and see if they increase your profit. Since the cost or risk of loss is minimal, you can see what others do, and then find out what works for you.

Somebody who has invested a large amount of money in an apartment complex, for example, will be all the more committed to seeing that the investment property turns a profit and can become very risk averse; so much so that they don't try techniques that could increase that profit because they are afraid of loss.

There is no shame in working hard and seeing to it that things work out for the best, but if you are unable to walk away from the investment and cut your losses, then you may stand to lose a whole lot more money than you should. Starting with a smaller property allows you to more accurately reassess whether investing in real estate is right for you. If you decide it isn't right, it will be easier to sell that rental home investment property than a more expensive apartment complex.

Purchasing and turning a profit on an investment property is just like any game you might play in life. To be successful, you must learn and completely understand the rules. Once you have the rules mastered, then you may go ahead and play your hand aggressively, but until then, it is in your best interest to take it slow and learn the ins and outs of the game. Starting out slow with a single, lower value investment property will help you stay alive in the real estate game longer and hopefully become a powerhouse down the line.

FIND A MENTOR

Another secret to success is that all successful property investors, in fact all high achievers in all fields, have one thing in common—they have a mentor. It puts them on the fast track to success because they benefit from the lessons learned by someone else and make fewer mistakes.

All the successful property investors I have dealt with over the years have hung out with like-minded investors and followed in the footsteps of the others who have already accomplished what they wanted to achieve. This helps them by being able to get advice on particular situations and kick around ideas for creative solutions. Often, their mentors will have encountered something similar previously and can quickly and easily point to a solution.

STAYING AFLOAT

Problems are only opportunities with thorns on them.

—Hugh Miller

Into each and every life, a little rain must fall. You have probably heard that saying, and it's true, especially when you step out and buy that first home or investment property. Not everything will go perfectly, but it can go much better than you imagine. Ninety-nine percent of dealing with challenges is about how you perceive them.

Because so many people look at real estate from the investment perspective, they can be very susceptible to negative information. Part of understanding yourself is knowing how you will react when the real estate market takes a little, or a big, dip. If you find yourself glued to the tube because of a report that the housing market is in a deep, dark slump in some areas, you have to step back and think about how you feel and why. Will you be calm, knowing that this is a normal part of the cycle, or will you immediately panic and stick a for-sale sign in your yard? The fearful investor will panic and sell out, while the cautious investor will adopt a wait-and-see attitude. Of course, some of the people who panic the most about the value of their homes are not real estate investors. They are normal, average people who have no plans to move, but still they are worried about the value of their home.

Declines of more than ten percent in the real estate market do happen on occasion. This does not happen very often, but it does happen, and it is part of the normal economic cycle. Even when there is talk of recession or hard times ahead, you must remember that when you have a home, you are in it for the long term, so any loss you may see is just on paper until you are ready to sell. While it is easy for me to say that, I also know that a home is also the biggest purchase that most people will ever make, and if you have a $250,000 home, then even a 10 percent decline is $25,000 of value. That's a lot. While it may make you uncomfortable, remember that it's only on paper right now. The only thing that keeps you from overreacting is having confidence in the market and becoming familiar with its occasional volatility.

There are several behaviors that can indicate that you are overly concerned about a market that is in a slump, and the first is to be obsessively focused on it. Are you turning on the financial news every few minutes to hear the latest from the floor of the exchange, or are you spending numerous hours clicking through every article on the Internet concerning the downturn? Constantly obsessing is actually just a sign of fear, and taking in more and more bad news each day does nothing but enhance your emotional turmoil. Wean yourself off of the constant analysis, and try to relax. Your money is in for the long haul, so what difference does it make if a particular company downgrades its fourth-quarter projections?

It is important to understand that the financial media, like any other source of media, looks for the stories that are going to offer the most interest for viewers. Unfortunately, this means that more often than not it involves some sort of scandal, financial bad news, or economic recession, all of which play on your emotional fears because you perceive that every bit of news they broadcast affects your investment in your home, and it does not. They are

So what should you look for when choosing a mentor, and what should you steer clear of?

There are lots of people out there calling themselves real estate experts, and many do a great job. The problem is that the recent property boom even made some below-average investors look like geniuses. Now that the tide has turned, many of these below-average or average investors will find themselves in trouble. My suggestion is to go back to the fundamentals when you choose whose ideas you will listen to and find someone who has seen some market fluctuations in the past.

You should look for people who at least have the following credentials and experience:

1. They must be investors themselves, currently actively investing in real estate, using the strategies they are teaching. This sounds like an obvious requirement, but you'd be surprised how many people spouting real estate strategies own none themselves. There is no room for theorists here. You must find someone who knows the business and has made money doing exactly the type of property investing that you want to learn.

2. They must have completed at least thirty real estate transactions so they have experience dealing with different buying and selling situations. Currently there are books and educational courses written by people who have purchased five or six properties. I would be wary of these individuals simply because that is not enough experience to have encountered a good variety of situations.

3. Somebody who has been hands-on investing for no less than twelve years, so they have had experience in different market conditions. Basically you want a survivor, not someone who has done it for a few years in good times but who has never had to make hard decisions.

They must have successfully used their strategies through a full property cycle. They've seen depressed markets, inflation, high interest rates and low interest rates, as well as changes in lending requirements and options.

4. Somebody who doesn't have a property to sell you. Now this isn't necessary in all cases, but it is just something to be aware of. You need to ensure that there isn't a potential conflict of interest. For this reason, you should be cautious with realtors and brokers. If they mentor you, then it would be a good idea to have an understanding that you won't buy real estate from them.

5. Somebody who is not appealing to your emotions, saying things such as act now or you will miss out, and somebody who doesn't put others down to make themselves look good. Look for somebody with integrity and a commitment to disclosure. There should be no rush and no good deals that can't be passed up. Wait until you are comfortable before taking any steps to make a purchase.

6. Don't be afraid to pay the right people to mentor you. If done right, your mentor will make money through joint activities with you. But a straight exchange of cash for information is fine, too.

7. Avoid somebody who is offering you something exciting, speculative, new, or the latest thing. Don't look for excitement in your investments. Your property investments are your way of securing your financial future. Don't be distracted from your long-term plans or strategies by promises of quick riches. Find the system that focuses on long-term wealth creation.

REVIEW

- Real estate is one of the best ways to accumulate wealth.

- When everyone else is selling, there are great deals to be made.

- Understand the mind-set of an investor.

- Property provides ongoing cash flow and long-term financial security.

- Risk is all about expectation.

- Find a mentor who can help solve problems and overcome challenges.

reporting the most interesting or sensational stories, not necessarily the most important for your particular situation, so do not allow yourself to get overwhelmed by everything you hear.

You should also know that just because some analyst or guru on TV says that you should be cautious with real estate, it does not mean that it is forever ruined, or that it applies to your particular area. They are just giving their opinion of the current overall general situation, and it changes all the time. There may also be other reasons that they have a particular opinion, depending on their personal background and experience. So it is always good to listen, but be slightly skeptical of anyone who thinks that they alone have the right answers. If they were always right, they would be millionaires themselves, but very few analysts or reporters are.

It is interesting that at the same time many people are overreacting to the market volatility and downturns in real estate, they are under-reacting to other areas of their financial lives. They accumulate more debt than they can manage and spend their money in even more frivolous ways. It is a strange and intriguing fact that as humans, when we worry about money, we also tend to do things that keep us from having it. Some people shop, some gamble, and some simply refuse to pay attention to where their money goes. Fear can be exceedingly motivating, but it can also lead to a type of paralysis that prevents us from truly understanding what we are doing and why. You must know when to take action to improve your financial health and when to stay the course. The problem is that the right answer can sometimes feel wrong.

In real estate investing, the timeline is long term. For this reason, when the market goes down, the best thing to do is to stay put or buy additional properties to rent. No matter how savvy you think you are, when you are actually faced with the situation, you may know the right answer, but putting in money or staying put when you see the numbers declining can feel so wrong. You may also start to second-guess yourself when all of your neighbors suddenly have for-sale signs in their yards. Remember, when almost everyone is going in one direction, you should probably go in the opposite direction. This is especially true with investments, be they real estate, or stocks, or whatever. When everyone is selling and trying to salvage short-term gains, you should be buying and take a long-term view. Once the real estate market rebounds—and it will—then you will make much larger gains than those who sold when the market went down.

Some investors think that they will pull out of their real estate now and then hop back in when the market goes up. This is called timing the market, and if it were that easy to do, then every investor would be a millionaire. The truth is that you are much more likely to lose money by hopping in and out of the market than just by consistently investing over time. This is true because the same fear that prods you to get out of volatile investments also prevents you from getting back in again until they are already on a high, so the only logical way they will go is down, and then you feel like you have to get out again. This is a vicious cycle that you should never allow yourself to fall into, as it will seriously damage your chances at long-term success.

FOREST FOR THE TREES

It is so easy to become wrapped up in the performance of any investment, especially if the market is making big moves either up or down. That does not give you an excuse to stop paying attention to the rest of your finances. There are literally millions of people struggling with an overload of debt or with an adjustable-rate mortgage that has reset to a much higher level. When faced with bad news about debt, the typical reaction is to freeze and want to do nothing, somehow hoping that it will ease up by itself or go away. You must be proactive with your real estate investments and take a realistic look at where you are, should circumstances change.

The first sign of this type of behavior is putting off one debt bill to pay another. Some would call this robbing Peter to pay Paul, and as debt load increases, it might seem like the only way to keep everything afloat. Unfortunately, it is by and large the beginning of a downward spiral, as debts continue to increase and your ability to pay them decreases. By the time you realize the enormity of the problem, it becomes overwhelming.

I normally advocate that everyone be as proactive as possible in these situations. If your credit card rate jumps, call the card issuer immediately, not a month or two down the road. If they do not lower the rate, look for another card. Do not wait until the balance gets so big that it affects your credit score.

The same is true of an adjustable-rate mortgage. You know well in advance if it is due to be reset. The time to negotiate with the lender is before the rate resets, so they are aware that you are willing to work with them. Trying to call and negotiate when you are thirty or sixty days late with a payment puts you in a much weaker position.

Although this book deals mainly with creating wealth through real estate, that goal is impossible unless your daily finances are under control and predictable. The time to correct any negative financial situation is immediately and efficiently, instead of waiting until your choices are limited. Feeling helpless and hopeless financially has forced many people to liquidate what little real estate equity they have, which decreases their wealth.

Another way that you can become blind to what is going on in the rest of your financial life is to become overconfident in your investments. If you happen to hit an upswing and have the value of your real estate investments rise very quickly, you may feel an excitement that leads you to believe that you are more experienced than you really are. It often helps to talk to a very experienced investor on occasion who may remember the tech stock bubble of the early 1990s, which rippled through California real estate, or the real estate downturn in the 1980s; this will give you a better perspective. We have all read or heard the disclaimer from financial companies that says, "Past performance is not a guarantee of future gain." This is a warning that no matter how good things look, you should be aware that it is more often than not temporary, and you are better to assume modest gains over many years than to try to hit the jackpot all at once.

As humans, we put the most belief in our recent experiences rather than relying on historical fact. This can get us into much trouble in the investment world. An investor can fall into the trap of feeling invincible, and when the fall comes, it can hurt.

RECOVERING FROM FINANCIAL DISASTER

There are many wide-ranging reasons for financial disasters that can feel like the end of the world. People lose their jobs, suffer the death of a spouse, or encounter a natural disaster such as a flood or hurricane. These things can completely disrupt the plans that they had for their lives. These things will eventually pass, but when you are knee deep in financial chaos, that can be of little comfort.

Even if it feels like your finances are barely on life support, you can recover from financial devastation and still plan to have some kind of retirement. The biggest problem that I run into with individuals who have struggled with money for whatever reason is their tendency to give up and quit trying. They think it is too hard and are convinced that they can't do it all. Other people must be smarter than they are or know some secret that they don't. None of this is true, but we create our own reality in our own minds, and until you realize that it's just as easy for you to make money as it is for the next guy, then you can really make some progress.

While there are many financial disasters that happen in your life, there are also the self-inflicted types of financial disasters. Have you ever known anyone who cashed out their retirement and other investments to start their dream business, only to have it fail? It happens. No one has a crystal ball, nor can they see exactly how a particular financial decision will turn out. We all make mistakes. If you have been through something like this, it can be even harder to think about investing in real estate because there is a tremendous amount of guilt associated with failing financially.

When recovering from a disaster of circumstance or a poor financial decision you many have made, it is important to understand that it is not an overnight process, and it does take time, but it can be done, and it rarely takes as long as you think it might. Awareness of the problem is the first step to developing a plan.

Even if you are doing well right now, life can be unpredictable, and a little preparation now can go a long way should you suddenly find yourself plunged into a full-scale crisis with severe financial consequences.

Also understand that the suggestions I am making are just that, as there are many paths that you can travel to get back on firm financial ground and start on the path to financial freedom through real estate.

THE BASICS

Should the worst happen, you first have to stop and evaluate your resources. Look not at what you think you might have but at what actually exists in hard numbers. Do you have an emergency fund? If so, how long do you have before it will run out? How many items in your budget can you do without until you have more income coming in? Will you have to liquidate some assets, and if so, which ones? This is very important if you hold real estate because it can't be liquidated immediately. You have to plan ahead and make decisions before things get desperate and you have fewer options.

Now you can look at other sources of assistance. You might be able to tap into the equity of a property or your primary home to help cover the shortfall. It might also be time to have an open and honest discussion with your family and include them in the process of setting spending priorities.

Their cooperation in trimming spending while you regroup will be essential to getting through a rough financial time and still hold onto that long-term dream of wealth. Adjusting to the fact that you cannot spend the way you used to is one of the biggest challenges in managing any financial crisis, but you cannot continue to live that former lifestyle until you have the income to go with it. Trying to keep up appearances will lead to more devastation. Create a plan for paying your essential bills and then cut back, eliminate, or postpone other expenditures.

As soon as you know that you will have limited resources, the best course of action with your creditors is to let them know. Many will allow you to set up a temporary plan, but you must contact them before you miss payments or make late payments. Determine an amount you can pay consistently until your finances improve, and then pay that regularly. It's important to be realistic. If you fail to follow through on your agreement, your creditors may seek other avenues for repayment.

Most financial downturns are much more temporary than they feel at the time, and by keeping your wits about you and not panicking, you can not only survive these instances but see opportunities that will make you even wealthier.

IT'S THE LITTLE STUFF

For most people, it is not one big financial event or disaster that gets them off track; it is a culmination of small decisions. It is the easy monthly payments that convince us that we can accumulate more stuff. It is the second car payment, boat payment, country club, and that time-share that you never visit. It is easy and common to become overcommitted, and rather than the instant effect of one specific financial event, it is a layering of seemingly small decisions that cause you to feel like you can't possibly invest, let alone invest in real estate. Here again, it is not the truth, but a reality that you have sold yourself, and you can choose not to believe it.

The problem is that many of the payments and expenses you take on without much thought are fixed and non-variable. They eat away at your bottom line each month, and you have fewer resources to draw on. It only takes one very small event at that point, even something as minor as a traffic fine, to destroy your financial house of cards.

Financial overcommitment has plagued almost everyone at some point. It is much like overeating; we all do it on occasion, but that does not mean that you have to continue down that path instead of building a future. There are numerous items that can bite you if you are not careful:

1. Buying a more expensive house than you can afford. Now it may seem odd that this would be at the top of the list in a real estate book, but it actually is one of the leading causes of financial overcommitment. Instead of looking at the home as an investment, buyers might look at it as an extension and want to get a more impressive home than they really need. This lessens their ability to have other money to invest. The real money is made when you buy a house, not when you sell it. You want a home that you can quickly and easily increase your equity in, so it will gain much more value in a shorter amount of time. You do not want the one that is priced at the pinnacle of the market because if the value decreases even slightly, it may take you years to really build up some good equity. Equity is not only your friend; it can make you wealthy quickly.

2. Car payments that stretch you to the limit. Everyone would like to drive the latest and greatest vehicle, and it can be incredibly easy to let the salesperson convince you that the payments are not that big, but the salesperson is not the one making the payment. These days, the actual payment for the car is not the only concern. Fuel efficiency is also a key factor. If you plan your life to the penny, a $.20 rise in gas prices can destroy your budget.

3. Keeping up with the neighbors. It is truly a cliché, but keeping up with the Joneses is a bad omen for your finances. This can include buying the right boat, having the right vacation home, sending the kids to the right private school, or belonging to the most exclusive clubs. All of these are lifestyle choices and can steal money from what could have been some significant investing and accumulating. It is important to evaluate why you are making particular choices, and if you realize it is for appearances, then understand that appearances will not pay your bills when you are age seventy-five.

4. The little things. Numerous small expenses that you accumulate and pay on an ongoing basis add up to more than you realize. Buying extended cable or satellite services when you spend little time in front of the TV can be unnecessary, as are some convenience expenses like house cleaning, lawn mowing, pedicures, or memberships. The point here is not to live like a pauper, but to evaluate what you use and need rather than habitually paying for things that serve no purpose.

The issue of overcommitment is compounded if you have large swings in income or if you receive large payments, as in seasonal work. Many commissioned salespeople fall into the category of overcommitment because they occasionally receive incredibly large checks and feel so wealthy—for a short time. When the cash is flowing freely, it is extremely easy to commit to more payments and a higher lifestyle than you can actually afford.

Learning to live on a set amount each month, no matter how high your actual income might be, is an especially important skill that can be learned, but sometimes it is a painful lesson. It is for this reason that self-employment can be difficult financially for some people. You must be incredibly committed to a financial plan and exceedingly disciplined in its execution. The tendency that we all have to spend exactly what we make hits dreadfully hard for the self-employed person, as that income is frequently uncertain and can have such dramatic swings.

DIGGING OUT

Once you recognize that you are overcommitted, there are only two effective plans of attack. One is to earn more money, and while this may temporarily relieve the problem, it will only work if you do not commit to even more once more cash comes in. For many people who are overcommitted, the real lesson to be learned is that they have to say no to the car, no to the pet grooming, and no to the big house. While some of these commitments may be easier to undo than others, if you stay overcommitted, then you will lose it all anyway. You must make the tough decisions.

Sometimes it is hard to know exactly how we get ourselves in so deep without noticing. It is much like the interesting fact that if you put a frog into a pot and heat it slowly, the frog will boil to death without even realizing it. That is certainly how it feels sometimes when your finances are out of control.

One way to create wealth is to create multiple sources of income, and real estate investment is one of those sources. Rental property makes you money around the clock, whether you are skiing in Banff or sunning yourself on a beach in the Caribbean. This is what you are striving for—a wealthy life, not one filled with debt and worry.

No matter what financial situation you currently are in, you can improve your life. You just have to choose. Choose to change those habits that don't serve to create long-term wealth, and refocus your thoughts on those habits and ideas that do. Leave behind the mind-set of appearances and buying more stuff, and instead put your money to work creating various streams of income that will allow you to live as you choose.

Chapter 9

REVIEW

- Real estate, like all investments, has cycles.

- Do not become obsessed with financial media news.

- Gurus and analysts that proclaim to know it all require a heavy dose of skepticism on your part.

- Real estate investing is for the long term, so short-term market volatility doesn't have that large an impact.

- Lead with common sense and know when you've financially overcommitted yourself.

- When disaster strikes, make an immediate plan for recovery and take action.

LOOK, MA, NO TOUPEE!

People do not lack strength, they lack will.

—Victor Hugo

The fact is that real estate is not a hard business to learn. Most all people go through the home-buying experience at some point in their lives. It isn't that big a leap from home buyer to investor if you are determined and willing to learn. You don't have to become a mogul like Donald Trump, but the option is there for you to take it as far as you want. It is your choice. I'm sure that you've already realized that the real secrets to becoming wealthy in real estate have nothing to do with which house you buy, but more to do with how much you believe in yourself.

It is easy to listen to those self-limiting beliefs we all have on occasion that say you can't do it or that it's not for you. And then, of course, there are those neighbors, friends, or coworkers who say that owning property is a giant pain, and that you really don't want to deal with it. Of course, they aren't any richer or better off than you are, so why in the world would you listen to what they have to say? The only way to achieve great results is to listen to those who have achieved great results and do what they recommend.

You may still be a little hesitant. That is normal but not profitable. Your existing beliefs, and the beliefs of those around you, can have a tremendous effect on how eager you are to try something new. They also affect how quickly you may give up. Let's look at a few of the more detrimental common beliefs and debunk them once and for all.

1. **I don't deserve to be rich.**

    Why not? Somebody has to be, right? Contrary to the beliefs of some, you can make a great deal of money by honest means and in turn do a great deal of good. What is wrong with making money, anyway? Wealthy people are often viewed with suspicion, as if they are engaged in criminal activity. Buying into this kind of thinking squashes your willingness to take opportunities that present themselves. Your feeling of deservedness has nothing to do with an amount of money. Therefore, it doesn't really stand in your way. You deserve all the abundance that this world has to offer, and denying yourself the chance at a good life does no one any good, especially you.

2. **Rich people are greedy.**

    Or selfish, uncaring, or insert your adjective of choice. I will clearly blame the media for this one. They pick the worst of the worst as far as the wealthy go and plaster their mugs all over TV and magazines. We love these kinds of trashy, tawdry stories, and it makes the publishers money. This makes it easy to assume that all rich people have these same qualities, when in reality they are the same as us. Most are good people who work hard. Some are irritating and annoying, but the same could be said about any clan. The rich are no different than you are; they just have more money. The rich have the capacity to fund great foundations that help millions of people around the world and keep people like you from having to foot the bill. One principle you could live by is this: you can't help the poor if you are poor yourself. Idealism is romantic, but reality is more sobering. Often, people mix the ideas of morality or spirituality and money. This is a variation of the belief that money is the root of all evil. What the Bible really says is that "the *love* of money is the root of all evil" (Timothy 6:10). These are two entirely different things, but the misinterpretation causes some people, even whole societies, to shun money. Become wealthy, and then start your own prosperity project and give away wealth to good causes of your choosing. As many charities say, be part of the solution, not part of the problem.

3. **You have to have a particular amount of money to be wealthy.**

   When would you consider someone wealthy? There is no set amount of money that makes you wealthy. It all depends on your perspective. True wealth is a state of mind, and it comes when you feel wealthy. This moment may be very different for different people. It may be that deep breath that you take as you stand on the balcony of your vacation home overlooking the sea. It may be when you wake up and see morning rush hour passing you by because your time is your own. It may be when a sports car sits in your garage. When you think wealthy, you feel wealthy, regardless of the exact amount of cash you have in the bank on any given day.

4. **Those with obvious material wealth must be rich.**

   Probably every one of us has seen a fabulous mansion, or a beautiful luxury car, and glanced at the owner, thinking, "It must be nice." Experience suggests that we get jealous or resentful for a whole multitude of reasons, and witnessing someone's material wealth is often one of them. But don't be so sure that the neighbor with the cool ATV, jet ski, swimming pool, and latest car is actually wealthy or even happy. He or she could be deep in debt to maintain the facade. Many people live the lifestyle, while constantly worrying about how to pay for it. The kind of wealth I encourage you to seek is real wealth, here you have a very positive net worth. Net worth is the value of all that you own minus what you owe. For many people, this number is negative, but you want to focus on increasing your net worth, not just taking on more debt. Anyone can present themselves as rich, but their net worth may actually be lower than yours, so don't be fooled.

5. **Money makes you happy.**

   Or money depresses you. Sounds confusing, doesn't it? Money doesn't have the power to do either. Money is paper and little round pieces of metal. It has no motives or intentions. There are happy poor people and miserable rich people. More money does help pay the bills, provided you know how to manage your wealth. But people with more money can also spend more than necessary and actually end up with less. We frequently hear of the celebrity or lottery winner who comes into tremendous wealth only to end up penniless a short time later. Money doesn't cure all problems or fix people; it only enhances the person you already are. If you are happy and care for others, then money will increase those traits. If you are rotten and treat others poorly, then money will enhance those qualities. Happiness is a choice that you make every day, no matter your financial circumstances.

6. **There's only so much money in the world.**

   This idea of scarcity is rampant among those who secretly wish they were wealthy. They think because they struggle for what they have, that there is limited wealth. This couldn't be further from the truth. Economists have said that there is more than enough money in the world for every single human being to live comfortably. It is also true that 3 percent of the people in the world hold 97 percent of all the wealth, and very few of these people inherited their wealth. We are paid according to the value that we offer to others, and some people give a tremendous amount of value. A good example is Bill Gates. He is a billionaire several times over because his ideas have completely altered the world we live in. Don't fall into the trap of believing that there's only so much money out there. There is an abundant supply, and you just need to claim what is already yours.

7. **Becoming rich is hard work.**

That the rich somehow work harder than you is a big misnomer. They work smarter, not harder. Each of us has the same twenty-four hours in each day. The richest person in the world still has the exact same amount of time that you do. But the wealthy understand the concept of leverage. They can't be everywhere, so they hire or go into business with others whose work earns them money. They do this repeatedly, leveraging their time to maximum advantage. Most of the world trades the hours of their day for a salary. The rich recognize that this is the fastest way to go broke. This is because it limits what you have the capacity to earn. You can become rich and not have to give up your life to do so. You just have to understand how it works. Many people think that if you work hard and save your money, you will become rich. This is a major untruth. While you can retire comfortably using this method, you will not retire rich. Setting back money and diversifying your investments are important concepts to learn, but they are only components of gaining wealth; they don't create the wealth.

8. **Earning lots of money makes you rich.**

This method works only if you actually save and invest the money that you make. If you spend it all, like some high-earning individuals do, then you will not be rich. Wealth is defined by net worth and investments, not by how much you earn from a job. In fact, people who earn more money but have no plan for the so-called disposable income end up doing just that— disposing of their income. Some do it out of guilt of having more than is necessary, others because they feel they owe it to themselves to have something nice, and still others spend their money to keep up with the Joneses. It really doesn't matter the reason because the result is the same. Earning money is easy; keeping it and putting it into investments that earn constant cash flow like real estate is another matter. Money flowing through your hands is one of the factors that may convince you that you don't have the extra money to invest, but we both know that you do. You just have to choose to keep the money and not let it burn a hole in your pocket.

9. **Being frugal is the way to wealth.**

    This is a big no! What this really does is set up an emotional environment of lack, causing you to miss out on opportunities to gain wealth because you become focused on every little penny. While you shouldn't throw money away, expenses are only one side of the equation, while creating multiple streams of income is the other. Though many financial gurus preach the gospel of cutting expenses, these are things not always within your control. If you trim your budget to the bone, and gas goes up $1 per gallon, what do you do? You've already cut your consumption, and there is nothing left to do but make more money to cover this problem. You will find this to be true repeatedly. Expenses sometimes just happen, and there is nothing you can do to avoid them. Constantly worrying over every dime only attracts more scarcity into your world, and that's never a good thing. Focus on creating wealth and be aware of what you spend, but don't obsess.

THE ESSENTIAL SKILLS

The secrets we have revealed contain some basic truths that you will want to carry with you. The first of those is that real estate investing is about relationships. People are your most valuable resource, and the more of them you know, the more likely you are to find good properties to buy, or buyers for your properties. When you encounter a challenge, the relationships that you cultivate with other investors can provide you with a pool of quality advisors. Treat people with respect and make it your goal to remember who you talk to and what they have to offer, even if you have to take notes. Now make it your goal to eventually be that sort of resource for others. Networking is essential for you to find the best opportunities.

You also must commit yourself to education. Any investment has a learning curve, and real estate is no different. Take classes, find a mentor, and learn from any mistakes that you make early on. When you go to a property, give yourself the tools to evaluate it properly, and keep emotions out of the mix. When you look at a rental property, for example, think about how certain changes would allow you to raise the income, and what that would do to the value long term. Having a feeling about a property, without understanding the numbers, gets many investors into trouble.

Realize that there is risk with everything, and risk is not necessarily bad. You must understand the risks with real estate and do what you can to mitigate those risks, such as having inspections, considering particular forms of financing, and other contingency clauses in the offer, so you'll get your deposit back should a deal fall through. Consider your exit strategy before you buy, and have a plan B. There are and will be many opportunities, and you simply must choose the best ones for your situation. Don't compare yourself to someone else or assume that you will never make an error; you will, but it's how you handle them that matters.

Prepare yourself to be a business person, and treat your real estate investing as a business. Have business cards, pen, and paper with you at all times. You never know when you'll see a property for sale or hear about one that you want to pursue. Sometimes, when you mention that you invest in real estate, sellers, buyers, and other investors suddenly appear with information, opinions, and sometimes even good deals. Be prepared, and expect that these people and opportunities will flow your way, and they will.

Create action-oriented goals, not just wishes. Frequently review your long- and short-term goals and hold yourself accountable. For example, require yourself to look at a certain number of properties per week, and maybe even to write a certain number of offers each month. Set goals for all sorts of little steps, like making six phone calls per week, checking online listings twice per week, and so on. Action creates momentum. Repeated action creates habits, and good habits lead to more successful real estate investing.

Understand that you will have ups and downs. We all have doubts and fears that can threaten to overwhelm us on occasion. Keep your mind in positive mode and don't allow it to feed on any negativity. Sometimes this can be difficult, especially if you must spend time with those who don't support your ideas and dreams. Realize that you are responsible for your emotions and reactions and that you choose if you allow others to affect you.

STEP INTO YOUR NEW LIFE

With the ideas I've presented within these pages, you have the information you need to get started changing your life. Whether you decide to invest in real estate or not, I hope the principles of goal setting and taking action have struck a chord with you. You have the ability to change your life, and the only thing standing in your way is for you to decide. There are real estate investing tricks and techniques that you may know or want to know. There are new ways of doing things that are worth learning.

The most important factor in your eventual success is the belief that you can accomplish anything that you set your mind to. Think back to the last vacation you planned. Were you excited and enthusiastic about all the details? Did you imagine where you would go and what you would do? Just like the excitement of planning a vacation, it takes sustained effort to manifest all your wants and maintain that excitement and passion.

People lose sight of their dreams because they spend more time worrying about the how or why they don't already have what they want. Their focus is misdirected. Some fall into the trap of fearing success and don't capitalize on their excitement and passion. They think that if they actually succeed, then they will have the responsibility to maintain a certain level of success. Others feel comfortable with being a great number-two person, staying out of the limelight and not sticking their own neck out. There is nothing wrong with living this way, if you are truly happy with it. However, if you want more, you must take a risk and get out of your comfort zone. You must allow your excitement to help you rather than denying its existence.

It's time to create a new belief system. Let go of and overcome your beliefs about how much you deserve and go for what you want. Creating a new belief happens by applying what you know. Develop new habits of positive self-talk. Before you know it, you will believe what you are saying and will have tangible results to back up your new belief system.

Fulfilling your purpose will require passion. "Purpose" has to do with our head—thinking about why we're here and understanding our calling. "Passion" has to do with our heart—the internal fire motivating and energizing us to fulfill our purpose. In the world we live in, natural passion is often a key to success and impact. Knowing information is valuable, but possessing the passion is invaluable. It is the deciding difference between successful and unsuccessful people in every field of endeavor. The passion on the inside affects everything on the outside. William Ward once said, "Enthusiasm and persistence can make an average person superior; indifference and lethargy can make a superior person average."

Passion is not something that is static or that stays the same. A fire either spreads or burns out. The tendency of fire, if left alone, is to go out. Passion works the same way. We need to work it, stoke it, and build it. There are many passion killers. A few common ones include complacency, difficult circumstances, an unbalanced lifestyle, and familiarity. The result is apathy. Apathy isn't a state of mind, it's a state of heart. The moment we lose our passion or zeal, we lose vision and perspective. The result is that we live lukewarm lives within the bounds of our comfort zone and never find out what could have been, though we often wonder. If you deny your dreams today and pretend that they don't exist, they might surface as regrets later. Guard the flame within you, and protect your passion.

The best way to maintain your excitement is to be around others who have the same perspective. Get involved in a mastermind group or employ a life coach. I refer to this as "filling the well." You can't feel upbeat if you are constantly stressed and overburdened with life. How many times have you gotten together with friends feeling totally exhausted, and after an hour or two of laughs, conversation, and ideas, you felt energized and ready to take on the world again?

Cut yourself some slack. Allow the time to refill your own well and treasure the time with those who energize and excite you. Over time this will be something you can do for others. Understand your purpose, and then seek to fulfill that purpose with passion and pursue it relentlessly. Focus your passion on fulfilling your purpose.

Take this opportunity to change and grow, serve and reach out. Living abundantly is about living with a sense of urgency and passion. It's living with a vision and a dream to give our lives to and achieving the goals that will forever change our lives.

No one said life was going to be easy. However, it doesn't have to be difficult, either. The fear of reality is always much more intense than reality itself. We imagine a much worse outcome than is even possible to make us feel better about staying right where we are and not changing.

We make our lives into whatever we choose. Actively embrace the life you have dreamed about. Pursue your wants with diligence. Never give up on yourself, no matter what challenges come your way.

REVIEW

- Real estate is an easy business to learn.
- You deserve all the abundance this world has to offer.
- Financial success allows you to do good for those you care about.
- Wealth is a state of mind, not an amount of money.
- Money will not make you happy.
- Don't worry about the "how," and step into your new life.